- You can return this item to any Bournemouth library but not all libraries are open every day.

- Items must be returned on or before the due date. Please note that you will be charged for items returned late.

- Items may be renewed unless requested by another customer.

- Renewals can be made in any library, by telephone, email or online via the website. Your membership card number and PIN will be required.

- Please look after this item - you may be charged for any damage.

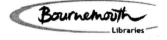

Bournemouth
Libraries

THE
SECRET AGENT'S
POCKET MANUAL

1939- 1945

THE
SECRET AGENT'S
POCKET MANUAL

1939- 1945

With an introduction and commentaries
by Dr Stephen Bull

BRITISH SPECIAL OPERATIONS EXECUTIVE
AMERICAN OFFICE OF STRATEGIC SERVICES

CONWAY

For Kerstin

First published in 2009 by
Conway
An imprint of Anova Books Ltd
10 Southcombe Street
London W14 0RA
www.conwaypublishing.com
www.anovabooks.com

A CIP catalogue record for this book is available from the British Library.

Publisher's Note
This facsimile compilation contains material of historic interest. The
techniques described herein must be considered in the context of their
original publication and the publishers exclude liability arising from
reliance on the information provided to the fullest extent of the law.

References to material not included in the selected extract have been removed
to avoid confusion, unless they are an integral part of a sentence. In these
instances the note [not included here] has been added.

ISBN 9781844861033

Printed and bound by 1010 Printing International Ltd, China

To receive regular email updates on forthcoming Conway titles, email
conway@anovabooks.com with Conway Update in the subject field.

CONTENTS

DUTCH RESISTANCE CARTOON

The discomfort of the conqueror atop the volcano of occupied Europe.
A key task of the secret agent was to make occupation as difficult as
possible. In France, divided initially into German occupied, Vichy, and
Italian occupied, and with Alsace and Lorraine quickly annexed by
Germany, the situation was already complex.

INTRODUCTION

There have been operations conducted by secret agents as long as there has been war – from the first attempts to creep up on an unsuspecting enemy to basic camouflage and simple ruses and sabotage. Rebellions against occupying forces occurred in biblical times, and sophisticated military espionage was well established by the seventeenth century. Bomb-throwing anarchists and spies such as Marta Hari helped usher in the violent twentieth century. Yet it is probably the 'secret armies' of World War II that grasp the popular imagination more than any other, and while, for the English-speaking world, British- and US-sponsored ventures into occupied Europe loom largest, these operations were conducted by citizens of all occupied territories in both the European and Far Eastern theatres. Some English-language espionage instruction manuals were quickly translated into other languages, such as French, Dutch, Polish, Norwegian, Serbo-Coat, Chinese and Malay.

Our fascination with the activities of these secret agents is fully justified – and three reasons for the significance of these particular missions are immediately apparent. The first is geographic, for, unlike World War I, when the German army was held in the West at Verdun and Ypres, Hitler's victorious Wehrmacht swept over much of Europe from the autumn of 1939 to late 1941. In addition to the conquest of France and Belgium, Denmark, Norway, and the Netherlands were all swallowed. The Czech lands and Austria had been seized and annexed respectively even before the fall of Poland, and later yet more territory would be taken in the Balkans. Italy was an early partner in crime, and several Eastern European states subsequently fell into line. These mind-boggling successes not only swelled Nazi ambitions to global proportions, but left populations of many millions occupied. A few resisted from the start: but for many more shock, humiliation, and disappointment turned more gradually to resentment, passive resistance, and finally active measures, as it became clear that the enemy war machine was being sustained by factories, food, and labour from all over Europe. Often hardship crept up incrementally – with shortages, labour conscription, ominous disappearances and increasingly iniquitous regulations piling upon each other.

The second reason for the great significance of secret operations in World War II is technological. For, as long as aircraft were feeble and short range, and radios large and inefficient, the possibilities for running successful undercover warfare at a distance were limited. However, once bombers could strike virtually anywhere, and radios could be hidden in suitcases, it became a different story. By the end of World War II it proved possible for resistance aircraft homing devices to be concealed in biscuit tins. Few places were now completely 'civilian' or fell genuinely 'behind the lines'.

Finally it has to be acknowledged that the war was ideological in a new way. Some saw it as national, but for the Nazis – increasingly as time progressed – the conflict became one of politics and race. Ultimately, in the mind of the Führer, the war became a battle of annihilation that the German people would either win or else disappear into total obscurity. In order to prevent their own annihilation, therefore, it thus became necessary for many civilians of all nationalities in occupied territories to become 'secret agents' to some degree, no matter how apparently insignificant. Churchill urged that Europe should be 'set ablaze' following the fall of France, but it has to be said that British subversive and clandestine activities got off to a slow, unfocused, and amateurish start.

EARLY BRITISH ESPIONAGE IN WORLD WAR II

The Secret Intelligence Service (SIS) – headed by an official, conventionally code-named 'C' – had been in existence since

1909, and already there were two branches involved in clandestine work. These were MI5, for counter intelligence and security, and MI6 for gathering intelligence. A new Section D, tasked with 'Destruction', was formed in 1938 under Major Lawrence Grand, and this succeeded in investigating German railways, and putting a few agents into the field. The War Office department GS (R), renamed MIR (Military Intelligence R) just before the war, also had a tiny staff working on aspects of clandestine warfare under Colonel J.C.F. Holland. The Royal Navy likewise had its own intelligence gatherers.

Another body formed in 1938 was EH, or 'Electra House' on the Embankment in London, a branch of the Political Intelligence Department with a remit for propaganda. EH supervised the printing of leaflets and, in theory, gave policy directives to the BBC – which was in practice already a larger and more experienced organisation attempting to maintain its authority by avoiding active misinformation. Although progress was modest in 1939, lines of responsibility were drawn between MIR and Section D, in which the former was assigned tasks that might be tackled by troops in uniform, and the latter was assigned undercover work that might be publicly deniable. Contacts were established in Bohemia, Scandinavia and Poland, whence Major Colin Gubbins of MIR had to make his escape at the time of the German invasion. Thought was also given to the need to help Allied personnel escape from enemy territory, overseen by MI9. There was also a foray to Romania – later recounted by Geoffrey Household, one of the participants – preparing an ultimately abortive attack on oil installations.

Perhaps the most important secret legacy of MIR would be the idea of the 'Auxiliary Units' – the nucleus of a British guerilla force. These would ultimately be regarded, for purposes of 'cover' and administrative convenience, as a part of the Home Guard. The 'Auxunits' operated from well-concealed underground shelters (technically Operational Bases or OBs), in groups of half a dozen to a dozen people, with stocks of munitions and food. Their job would have been to harass invaders, cut communications and, if necessary, be the beginning of full-blown guerilla war. Later a secret training establishment for the Auxunits was set up at Coleshill House near Swindon, and a sabotage instruction book was issued under a false cover bearing the title *Countryman's Diary, 1939*. Guerilla techniques were also taught to the wider Home Guard, often in 'battle schools' through the auspices of experts who had fought in the Spanish Civil War – notable practitioners included Bert Levy, author of the 1941 *Guerilla Warfare*, Tom Winteringham, and John Langdon-Davies.

The crisis of Dunkirk in 1940 jolted politicians, spies, and bureaucrats alike out of any lingering complacency. Though many of the pre-existing secret sections would be retained, the need to bring together the multiple arms of sabotage and organised resistance to work abroad together in one much-expanded body was recognised. As Hugh Dalton, Minister for Economic Warfare, reported to Lord Halifax on 2 July:

> We have got to organise movements in enemy occupied territory comparable to the Sinn Fein movement in Ireland, to the Chinese Guerillas now operating against

---

[OPPOSITE] NO. 74 'STICKY' BOMB

Developed in the UK in 1940 the 'Sticky Bomb' was a potent, if alarming, anti-tank grenade full of nitro-glycerine. The metal covering fell away when a pin was pulled, and the bomb could then be thrown or banged onto the surface of the tank where it stuck: five seconds later it exploded. It was supplied to the 'Auxunits' and European resistance forces. Other grenades used by clandestine fighters in Western Europe included the ubiquitous 'Mills Bomb', the plastic explosive filled 'Gammon grenade', and bombs from old French army stocks. At the end of the war OSS also produced the 'Beano', a spherical explode-on-impact type.

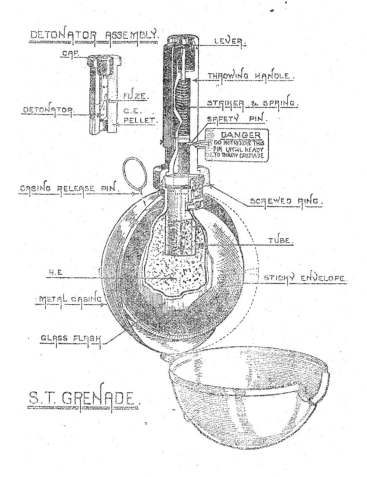

DETONATOR ASSEMBLY.

CAP.

DETONATOR.

FUZE.

C.E. PELLET.

LEVER.

THROWING HANDLE.

STRIKER & SPRING.

SAFETY PIN.

DANGER
DO NOT REMOVE THIS
PIN UNTIL READY
TO THROW GRENADE

CASING RELEASE PIN.

SCREWED RING.

TUBE.

H.E.

STICKY ENVELOPE.

METAL CASING.

GLASS FLASK.

S.T. GRENADE.

Japan, to the Spanish Irregulars who played a notable part in Wellington's campaigns or – one might as well admit it – to the organisations which the Nazis themselves have developed in almost every country of the world.... It is quite clear to me that an organisation on this scale and of this character is not something which can be handled by the ordinary departmental machinery of either the British Civil Service or the British military machine. What is needed is a new organisation to co-ordinate, inspire, control and assist the nationals of the oppressed countries who must themselves be direct participants. We need absolute secrecy, a certain fanatical enthusiasm, willingness to work with people of different nationalities, complete political reliability.

THE BIRTH OF THE SOE

Somewhat bizarrely this new and avowedly 'no-holds-barred' organisation was ushered into existence by none other than Neville Chamberlain, who had recently resigned as prime minister, but still acted as Lord President of the Council. His paper of recommendation christened the fledgling 'Special Operations Executive' – or SOE. Hugh Dalton would be its political control. The War Cabinet approved this on 22 July 1940: Gladwyn Jebb was given the title of Chief Executive Officer and Sir Frank Nelson was appointed to run SOE, while Grand and Holland were shuffled off to other duties. Theoretically SOE was to have three wings, SO1, 2 and 3, covering propaganda, active operations and planning respectively, though things did not pan out nearly so neatly in practice. SO1, for example, lasted less than a year, being given its independence as the Political Warfare Executive or PWE in which Sefton Delmer, Donald McLachlan and Ellic Howe would be key movers. As political overseer, Lord

Selborne took over from Dalton in 1942, and promptly replaced Nelson with Sir Charles Hambro – and Colin Gubbins came back into the picture as executive director of SOE under the code name 'M'.

Though it started small, SOE would eventually be large and dispersed over many secret locations. Much of the organisational brain was located in London offices at Baker Street and Gloucester Place. Millis Jefferis, a former member of 'MI' who now headed SOE's development and supply of special devices, was in Portland Place and 'display' facilities for his wares were in the Natural History Museum at South Kensington. When bombed out of Portland Place, new accommodation was found out of town at Whitchurch, at Station IX, Welwyn Garden City, Station XII near Stevenage and, from 1942 Station XV at Barnet. Further bases, often country houses in South-East England, were 'schools' fulfilling recruitment and training functions. Further afield there was a Scottish training area, and a 'cooler' in the Highlands, used mainly to store agents who were required to be kept incommunicado until they could safely be returned to normal service life. There were also headquarters abroad, of which one of the most significant was in Cairo.

Individual sections of SOE were devoted to activity in specific countries, and France was significant enough to merit six sections. Amongst these were F staffed by independents; RF by Gaulists; AMF which was based in Algiers, and DF dealt with escape. SOE reached its maximum personnel establishment in mid-1944 when about 13,000 strong: perhaps a third of these were agents, the remainder being planners, trainers, security, research, supply, signals and general administration staff. Many, but not all, were drawn from the personnel of existing services – though naturally recruitment focused on people with relevant language skills and backgrounds. About a third of SOE was female, and again quite a few were drawn from the services or

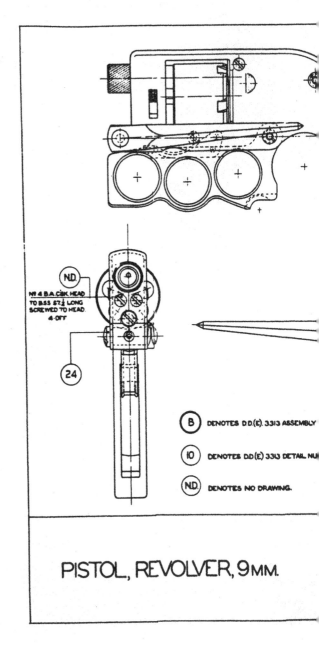

N.D.

Nº 4 B.A. CSK. HEAD
TO B.S.S. 57¼ LONG
SCREWED TO HEAD.
4·OFF

24

(B) DENOTES D.D.(E). 3313 ASSEMBLY

(10) DENOTES DD.(E) 3313 DETAIL NU

(N.D.) DENOTES NO DRAWING.

PISTOL, REVOLVER, 9MM.

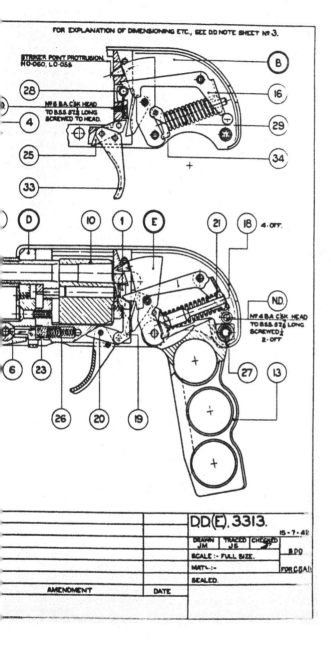

FOR EXPLANATION OF DIMENSIONING ETC., SEE D.D. NOTE SHEET N° 3.

STRIKER POINT PROTRUSION.
HI-0·060, LO-0·55

N° 6 B.A. CSK. HEAD
TO B.S.S. 57½ LONG
SCREWED TO HEAD.

4. OFF.

N° 4 B.A. CSK. HEAD
TO B.S.S. 57¼ LONG
SCREWED ½
2. OFF

		DD(E). 3313.			
				15 · 7 · 48	
		DRAWN JM	TRACED JS	CHECKED	
		SCALE :- FULL SIZE.			S DO
		MAT'L.:-			FOR C.S.A.I.
		SEALED.			
AMENDMENT	DATE				

INTRODUCTION 15

*British experimental 'Pistol, Revolver, 9mm': plan dated 15 July 1942.
It is uncertain whether this design saw action, but it encapsulated
many features suitable for clandestine use. It was chambered for 9mm
Parabellum rounds, which also fitted the Sten gun and enemy weapons.
The short barrel and folding trigger were tried and tested space savers,
but the butt also folded, and the revolving cylinder accommodated only
five rounds, allowing for a flatter profile when stowed away. When folded
and held by three fingers through the holes in the grip, it became a
weighty knuckle duster. A short, but vicious looking, folding bayonet
converted the revolver to a stabbing weapon.*

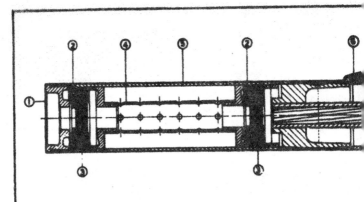

1. Silencer Tube End Cap.	11. Striker Pin Spring.
2. Steel Baffle Plate.	12. Backsight.
3. Rubber Baffle (self-closing).	13. Breech Operating Handle.
4. Forward Silencer Unit.	14. Positive Safety Catch.
5. Silencer Tube.	15. Hand-operated Safety Catch.
6. Foresight.	16. Magazine Spring.
7. Bursting Chamber.	17. Magazine and Pistol Grip.
8. Barrel.	18. Magazine Retaining Catch.
9. Extractor.	19. Trigger.
10. Striker Pin.	20. Trigger Guard.

WELROD   9 M[M]

No firearm achieves absolute silence, and most are more accurately described as 'sound moderated'. Nevertheless the Welrod was one of the quietest of the Second World War, having both a system of baffles and a relatively low velocity. Its name derived from Welwyn (Garden City), where it was devised. The magazine held five rounds, but the pistol needed cocking after each shot. It was used by both SOE and OSS in the latter part of the war. Other sound-moderated arms on the Allied inventory included the De Lisle carbine, which combined parts from the Lee Enfield rifle and Colt semi automatic pistol, and the High Standard .22. OSS also experimented with the 'Little Joe' and 'William Tell' cross bows.

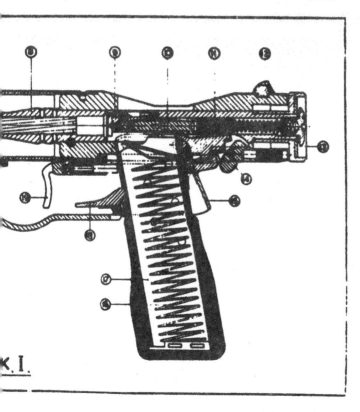

K.I.

enlisted with the First Aid Nursing Yeomanry by way of cover. Whilst some have indiscriminately referred to the clandestine warriors of Britain and the US as 'spies' – and indeed many were executed by the Germans as such – the proper name, often rightly insisted upon by veterans, was 'agent'.

THE OSS AND OTHER US INTELLIGENCE ORGANISATIONS

Like the United Kingdom, the United States had several different intelligence bodies prior to World War II. These included the Office of Naval Intelligence; the War Department's Military Intelligence Division, also known as G2; and the FBI whose domestic remit was expanded to cover Latin America in 1940. Only in July 1941 was a new White House agency established to 'collect and analyse' all information and data pertaining to national security under the COI or Co-ordinator of Information. The man heading this effort was the war hero and millionaire Wall Street lawyer, William Joseph Donovan. By October 1941 the COI had New York and London offices; a Radio News operation; a Research and Analysis section divided into five divisions and separate areas of foreign

[OPPOSITE] US LIBERATOR PISTOL

Pictorial instruction sheet to accompany the US 'Liberator' .45 pistol, 1942. Designed as a result of an idea emanating from the Psychological branch of the National Research Defence Committee, the Liberator, also jokingly known as the 'Woolworth Gun', was one of the crudest, cheapest, weapons of the Second World War. The concept was childishly simple: create an easy to conceal mass production firearm, and drop it in huge numbers to dissatisfied occupied populations. The cartoon instruction sheet was actually something of a triumph since it meant that the gun could be deployed anywhere – the language of the user and his or her degree of literacy was irrelevant.

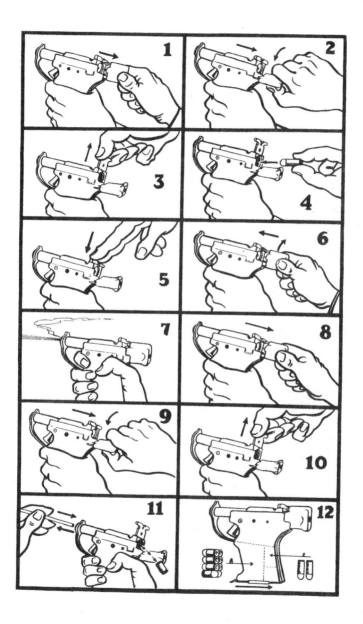

interest; and a Visual Presentation section, which prepared digests of intelligence and included a reference library.

After the American entry into the war the far more proactive role of the organisation would be reflected in the change of title to Office of Strategic Services or OSS, under the newly formed Joint Chiefs of Staff, in June 1942. Again in a parallel with what had happened in Britain, the existing Foreign Information Service was taken away from the organisation and a separate Office of War Information embracing 'white' propaganda was created. OSS now took on all aspects of clandestine warfare, and eventually encompassed divisions for research and analysis; development; counter-espionage; special operations; secret intelligence; and actual Operational Groups aimed at different countries. The SO branch was consciously close to SOE in its remit, being charged with sabotage and liaison with underground anti-occupation movements. Under Morale Operations were included not only disguised 'black' propaganda, but such delights as bribery; counterfeiting; abduction; and attempts to manipulate black markets. Though there were areas of disagreement, the relationship between OSS and SOE was undoubtedly symbiotic. SOE had a useful head start and helped to train OSS operatives at its Canadian Camp X school on Lake Ontario: later SOE benefited from US supplies and intelligence.

Recruit Training Centre 11, on a country estate twenty miles from Washington, was one of the key OSS facilities in the US. Here recruits were taught intelligence-gathering methods, covers, and the use of 'cut outs' – or intermediaries who could create links with sub-agents. Realistic outdoor training facilities A, B and C were in Virginia and Maryland. An assessment centre for volunteers was also established on the West Coast. Mission headquarters were eventually established overseas in Algeria; Italy; India; China; and, perhaps surprisingly, Switzerland. Operational Groups also attached themselves to the headquarters of US armies in Europe at the end of the war. Hardware research and development fell under the purview of the National Defence Research Committee, Division 19 – which was responsible for 'miscellaneous' matters. The key facility was the Maryland Research Laboratory, or MRL, under Dr Stanley Lovell, which devoted itself to problems submitted by OSS. Lovell reported directly to 'Wild Bill' Donovan. In addition to its Technical division, research and development activity also encompassed three other fields. Camouflage included clothing and other personal items, as well disguised objects; Documentation covered forged papers, printing and badges; and Special Assistants. This last was a euphemism for drugs, including suicide pills, temporary 'knock-out drops' and 'truth' drugs.

Though some agents were spirited in and out of neutral countries, or arrived by sea, the usual method of delivery for North-West Europe was by air. The RAF used three main types of aircraft to land at improvised airfields, the Lysander, Hudson and eventually Dakota. Of these the Westland Lysander was the most suitable, being small and capable of landing on short strips. Speed was of the essence, and a turnaround time on the ground of two or three minutes was by no means unusual. A variety of other craft were used for parachutists, perhaps most famously the B-24 Liberators of the USAAF 'Carpetbagger' squadrons. Their busiest month was July 1944 when they dropped more than 7,000 containers and packages, 1,378 bundles of leaflets, and 62 agents.

THE EFFICACY OF SECRET AGENTS

It has to be admitted that while there were dramatic successes, SOE and OSS also had bloody failures. Probably the worst was the so-called 'Englandspiel' in the Netherlands in which a whole network was wound-up by the enemy. SOE operatives Thys Taconis and H Lauwers were double-crossed by what the Germans called *Vertauensmänner* – their own local agents, who were pretending to be Dutch resisters. Once arrested Lauwers agreed to co-operate, but deliberately omitted security checks in his messages back to London so that SOE would be alerted. Tragically this quick thinking was ignored and many agents were now air-dropped to join the apparently thriving network, only to go to their deaths. Only when two – code named 'Cabbage' and 'Chive' – managed to escape from a concentration camp was the alarm raised. Even then, a phoney message from the Netherlands protested that Cabbage and Chive had gone over to the enemy and were not to be trusted.

ABOUT THIS BOOK

Over the course of the war both SOE and OSS – and their methods and equipment – increased markedly in professionalism and scope. Perhaps surprisingly quite a few aspects of their work were written up during the war, and essentially it is these manuals and papers that provide the raw material for the chapters that follow. The selection of texts is broadly chronological, each prefaced with its own brief introduction. It is worth noting that for the most part such paperwork was not taken into the field, nor was it created for the edification of future generations: it was produced either for an internal administrative purpose, or as home training literature. Some of the manuals served effectively as catalogues for planners and agents, who were thus informed what stores and techniques were already to hand. Others formed the basis for the detailed planning of actual operations. The main categories of material that did reach 'the front line' were booklets of techniques, commonly in translation, for the training and information use of local resistance groups, and propaganda items, often in German, which were targeted at enemy-held areas.

STAMP COMMEMORATING REINHARDT HEYDRICH (1904–42)

Operation Anthropoid – the assassination of SS Obergruppenführer
Reinhardt Heydrich, Deputy Reich Protector for Bohemia and Moravia – was
a joint mission of SOE and the Czech government in exile. Agents Jan Kubis
and Joseph Gabcik were trained in the UK and dropped by parachute. They
attacked Heydrich's car in Prague on 27 May 1942, and though Gabcik's
Sten gun jammed, Kubis threw a grenade. The wounded Heydrich died
eight days later. In reprisal the villages of Lidice and Lezaky were raised and
over 2,000 people executed. The stamp depicting Heydrich was official, but
Allied black propagandists produced a fake stamp of Himmler the following
year, which was distributed in neutral countries to bolster the suggestion that
the Reichsführer was preparing to replace Hitler.

The endpapers and two plate sections of illustrations of equipment are drawn from the two volumes of the British 'Top Secret' publication *Descriptive Catalogue of Special Devices and Supplies*, issued in 1944 and 1945. This replaced an earlier *Catalogue of Supplies*, produced in September 1943. Interestingly the *Descriptive Catalogues* were originally compiled in a looseleaf format so that new matter and amendments could easily be inserted – they were thus dynamic working reference documents. Originals are retained in the National Archives at Kew, London.

The ingenuity displayed in the creation of these secret agents' toys is matched only by the bravery demanded by their use – for these, often innocuous looking, objects were the real stock in trade of sabotage, assassination, revolt, intelligence and secret communication.

PARTISAN LEADER'S HANDBOOK, 1939

PRINCIPLES OF GUERILLA WARFARE AND SABOTAGE

British Military Intelligence

The *Partisan Leader's Handbook*, compiled by Major Colin Gubbins of Military Intelligence R in 1939, may be considered one of the starting points of British secret operations in World War II. Together with *The Art of Guerilla Warfare*, also by Gubbins, and a booklet on explosives by Millis Jefferis, these three bibles of the unconventional were produced in response to an order by Lord Gort to Colonel Holland to create what he called a 'Field Service Regulation' for guerillas. Top secret at the time of their production, these documents nevertheless achieved almost universal circulation in both Europe and South-East Asia. They were eventually translated into a multitude of languages including, not only the obvious choices of French, Dutch, Polish, Norwegian, and Serbo-Coat, but Chinese, Malay, and others. In the postwar world some of these documents would ultimately come back to haunt the establishment that produced them.

The vision encapsulated here has become recognisable as the modus operandi of the guerilla the world over: harass the enemy by any means; sever enemy communications; employ mobility and the support of the local population; do not act until confident of success. So ruthless and chilling is some of the advice offered that, after the enemy surrender, at least one German accused of war crimes cited it as justification for his own actions. Nevertheless it is also worth pointing out that in many of the essentials, Gubbins merely collected and interpreted examples of behaviour being used against British forces in various parts of the Empire in the 1930s. In the event, partisans in Western Europe did use many of these hit-and-run tactics. Only with D-Day did some of these resisitance fighters emerge for full-blown battle, as in the Vercors near Grenoble, where 3,000 fought aided by an SOE team under Richard Heslop.

1. Remember that your object is to embarrass the enemy in every possible way so as to make it more difficult for his armies to fight on the main fronts. You can do this by damaging his rail and road communications, his telegraph and postal system, by destroying small parties of the enemy, and in many other ways which will be explained later.

Remember that everything you can do in this way is helping to win freedom again for your people.

2. You must learn the principles of this type of warfare, which are as follows:

(a) Surprise is the most important thing in everything you undertake. You must take every precaution that the enemy does not know your plans.

(b) Never engage in any operation unless you think success is certain. Break off the action as soon as it becomes too risky to continue.

(c) Every operation must be planned with the greatest care. A safe line of retreat is essential.

(d) Movement and action should, whenever possible, be confined to the hours of darkness.

(e) Mobility is of great importance; act therefore where your knowledge of the country and your means of movement – i.e., bicycles, horses, etc. – give you an advantage over the enemy.

(f) Never get involved in a pitched battle unless you are in overwhelming strength.

(g) Never carry incriminating documents on your person nor leave them where they can be found.

The whole object of this type of warfare is to strike the enemy, and disappear completely leaving no trace; and then to strike somewhere else and vanish again. By these means the enemy will never know where the next blow is coming, and will be forced to disperse his forces to try and guard all his vulnerable points. This will provide you with further opportunities for destroying these small detachments.

3. Types of Operations – Operations can be divided into two main types: –

(a) Those of a military nature which entail the co-ordinated action of a certain number of men under a nominated leader.

(b) Individual acts of sabotage, of sniping sentries, etc., for which men can be specially selected to work individually in certain areas.

For action of a military nature the choice of suitable leaders is of great importance. A leader must have courage and resource, he must be intelligent and a good administrator and be a man of quick decision. He must know intimately the country in which he is operating, and should be able to use a compass and map. The sort of man required is the type whom other men will willingly accept to lead them in dangerous actions, and whose personality will hold them together.

The size and composition of guerilla parties must depend on the nature of the country and the hold which the enemy has over it. It must be remembered that the speed of modern communications, i.e., motors, wireless, etc., and the presence of aeroplanes make it very difficult for a large party to remain concealed for any length of time. Parties should therefore number between 8 and 25, depending upon the work to be done; such parties can move quickly and yet hide themselves fairly easily. Under specially favorable conditions, it may be possible to collect several parties together, up to 100 men or more, for some important undertaking. In such cases, however, the arrangements for dispersal after the operation must be made with special care.

4. Modern large-sized armies are completely dependent on roads, railways, signal communications etc., to keep themselves supplied with food, munitions and petrol, without which they cannot operate. These communications therefore form a most suitable target for guerilla warfare of all kinds, and any attack on them will at once force the enemy to disperse his forces in order to

guard them. Communications are open to attacks both of the military and sabotage type. Attacks can also be directed against small detachments of the enemy, stocks of food, munitions, etc., and many other objects.

5. Military action is employed when it appears that damage can only be inflicted if force has to be used first.

The following are types of military actions: –

(a) Destruction of vital points on roads, bridges, railways, canals, etc., when action by an individual employing secret means would not be effective. If a hostile guard has first to be overpowered, or work preliminary to destruction requires a considerable number of men, the project must be undertaken as a military operation.

(b) The raiding and destruction of hostile mails, either in lorries or trains.

(c) The destruction of enemy detachments and guards.

(d) The organization of ambuscades of hostile troops and convoys travelling by road or train.

(e) The destruction of stocks and dumps of food, petrol, munitions, lorries, etc., by first overpowering the guards on them.

(f) The seizure of cash from hostile pay-offices etc.

ETC. ETC.

6. Military action is greatly facilitated by the support of the local population. By this means, warning can be obtained of all hostile moves, and it will not be possible for the enemy to carry out surprise action. It is therefore important to endeavour not to offend the people of each district, but to encourage their patriotism and hatred of the enemy. Successful action against the enemy will breed audacity and force the people to take note and respond. Their response in the first instance should be directed to the supply of information about the enemy, his strength, movements, etc., and to assistance in the concealment of compatriots who are taking part in guerilla warfare. In effect, the people must be taught to boycott the

hostile troops completely, except as may be necessary to obtain information. This can best be done by convincing them that the enemy's occupation is only temporary, that he will soon be ejected, that those of the people who have helped will then be rewarded, but that those who have fraternized with the enemy will be ruthlessly punished. The question of 'informers' and traitors who are in league with the enemy is dealt with later.

7. The areas most suitable for military action are those where cover, such as rocks, trees, undergrowth, etc., give a concealed approach to the object or detachment to be attacked. Such cover not only provides an opportunity for attack without discovery, but also for getting away safely when the attack is completed. In all such attacks, it is important that sentries should be posted on all approaches to give warning of any possible surprise by the enemy; it is not necessary that all these sentries should be armed men, in fact it will frequently be of advantage to use some women and children, who are less likely to be suspected. A simple code of signals must be arranged.

Every operation of this nature must be most carefully planned. When some particular operation has been decided upon, the locality must be thoroughly reconnoitred, and the enemy's movements in the vicinity should be systematically studied and noted over a period of days, with special reference to such points as the following, where applicable: –

    (a) Hours when sentries are relieved, and how relief is carried out.

    (b) Total strength of guard or detachment.

    (c) How and when do supplies for the guard arrive? Are civilians allowed to enter the post?

    (d) Where do men not on sentry-go keep their rifles? Are these rifles chained up or in plain racks?

    (e) Are men allowed to leave the position for short periods?

    (f) How often are guards inspected, by whom and at what times?

    (g) What means of communication for the post exist, i.e., telegraph, motor-cycle, or cycle messengers, carrier pigeons, etc. Can these be destroyed?

(h) Do mails or small detachments of men follow regular routes at fixed times, giving opportunities for ambushing?

(i) Do these detachments have sentries, advance parties, etc., or do they proceed in one group?

(j) Are motor vehicles fitted with bullet-proof or puncture-proof tyres, armoured sides, etc.?

(k) What special tools and explosives, if any, are required for the operation, and what amount?

Examples of such operations are given at the end of the book.

8. Sabotage deals with the acts of individuals or small groups of people, which are carried out by stealth and not in conjunction with armed force. These undertakings, however, frequently produce very valuable results and, like military action, force the enemy to disperse his strength in order to guard against them. The following are examples of this type of work: –

(a) Jamming of railway points.

(b) Destructive work on roads, railways, canals, telegraphs, etc., where this can be done by stealth.

(c) Firing of stocks of petrol; burning garages, aeroplane hangars, etc.

(d) Contamination of food, of forage, etc., by acid, by baccilli, poison, etc.

(e) Contamination of petrol by water, sugar, etc.

(f) Destruction of mails by burning, acids, etc.

(g) Shooting of sentries.

(h) Stampeding of horses,

(i) Use of time bombs in cars, trains, etc.

ETC. ETC.

9. Sabotage to be effective requires the same degree of careful preparation as does military action. The first point is to choose an objective which has some value, even if it is only the sniping of a sentry or the firing of a stack of forage. Such shootings mean that the enemy must double his sentries or risk their loss; such destruction means more guards. So more troops have to be used, and this is one of your objects.

The next step must be to study the place and conditions, so that the most favourable moment for success can be selected. A sure line of retreat, or an alibi, must be arranged beforehand. Often, it will be necessary to wait a fortnight or longer before the right opportunity presents itself. At the same time, however, it may be necessary at times to carry out sabotage on the spur of the moment without previous preparation, for example when a convoy of lorries arrives unexpectedly in a village, and there is a chance of setting one on fire. Such opportunities should not be missed. It is certain that the enemy will force a proportion of the inhabitants to work for him in mending roads, loading and unloading trucks, and other works of a military nature. Such working parties provide good opportunities for sabotage by time bombs, by acids and other devices.

10. Organization: –

(This particular pamphlet is intended simply for the use and instruction of guerilla 'parties.' The higher organization of guerilla warfare throughout a whole country or region is dealt with in the manual "The Art of Guerilla Warfare" [not included here]).

In the early stages of guerilla activities, before hostile counter-measures have become intense, it will be possible for the members of a party to live independently in their own villages and homes and carry on their normal occupations, only collecting when some operation is to be undertaken. The longer they can go on living in this way the better. When the enemy begins to take active measures to prevent guerilla warfare by raids on suspected houses, by arresting suspects, etc., it will eventually be necessary for the guerillas to 'go on the run' – i.e., to leave their houses and live out in the country, hiding themselves by day, and moving at night. The number of men 'on the run' in any one party must depend on the nature of the country'. If it is wild, hilly, and forested, it may be possible for parties of up to 100 strong to avoid detection for long periods. If the country is flat and featureless and cultivated, it may be difficult for even one man to remain undetected for long. The organization must therefore depend on the country; the wilder it is the closer can the organization be – i.e., the leader has his men closely under control all the time, and the party moves from place to place, as necessary, to carry out operations or avoid capture. In less favourable country, the organization must be looser, and men must be collected for action by secret means. If and when the enemy's activities make it too dangerous, for the time being, to continue, the men should leave their area, and join parties operating in more favourable conditions. These latter parties must always serve as a rallying point for men who have been forced by danger of arrest to 'go on the run', for deserters from the enemy, and escaped prisoners.

The "leader" is responsible for the organization; the importance of selecting only men who are reliable and resourceful is thus paramount.

11. Information: – If you can keep yourself fully informed of the enemy's movements and intentions in your area, you are then best prepared against surprise, and at the same time have the best chance for your plans to succeed. The enemy is handicapped in that his men must wear uniforms and are living in a hostile country, whereas your agents wear ordinary clothes and belong to the people and can move freely among them. Therefore, make every use of your advantage in order to obtain information. Suitable people must be selected from among the inhabitants to collect information and pass it on; these should be people who are unfit for more active work, but whose occupations or intelligence make them specially suitable for the task. The following are types who can usefully be employed: –

  (a) Priests.
  (b) Innkeepers.
  (c) Waitresses, barmaids, and all café attendants.
  (d) Domestic servants in houses where officers or men are
       billeted. These are a very useful source.

(e) Doctors, dentists, hospital staffs.

(f) Shopkeepers, hawkers.

(g) Camp followers.

These people must be trained to know what sort of information is required; this is most easily done by questioning them on further points whenever they report anything, as they will then learn to look for the details required (see example at the end of the book). They must also be trained to be on the look-out for enemy agents disguised as compatriots.

It is important that as little as possible of this information should be in writing, or, if it is in writing, that it should not be kept any longer than necessary. All papers, documents, etc., dealing with intelligence or your organization in any way, must be destroyed immediately you have finished with them, or kept in a safe place until destroyed.

It has been proved over and over again in guerilla warfare that it is the capture of guerilla documents that has helped the enemy most in his counter-measures. These have been captured either on the persons of guerillas, or seized in houses that have been raided. The utmost care is therefore necessary.

12. Informers: – The most stringent and ruthless measures must at all times be used against informers; immediately on proof of guilt they must be killed, and, if possible, a note pinned on the body stating that the man was an informer. This is the best preventive of such crimes against the homeland. If it is widely known that all informers will be destroyed, even the worst traitors will hesitate to sink to this depth of perfidy, whatever the reward offered.

If a person is suspected of being an informer, he can be tested by giving him false information, and then seeing if the enemy acts on it. If the enemy so acts, such evidence is sufficient proof of guilt, and the traitor must be liquidated at the first opportunity.

13. Enemy Counter-Measures and their frustration: – The best means of defeating the enemy's counter-measures is by

superior information which will give warning of his intentions –
i.e., of raids against suspected houses, of traps he may lay, of
regulations he proposes to enforce in the territory he occupies, etc.
Attempts to bribe the people must be met by the measures shown
in paragraph 12 above.

Certain counter-measures, however, can only be met by special
action; for instance, the use of identity cards, which the enemy is
certain to introduce when guerilla warfare becomes active, in order
to assist him in tracing the guerillas. It will then be necessary to
obtain or copy the official seals and stamps so as to provide
identity cards for the guerillas.

When the enemy finds that passive means are insufficient to
defeat guerilla operations, he will resort to active measures. These
will probably take the form of mobile columns of considerable
strength, horsed or in motors, including armoured cars and tanks,
with which he will make sudden sweeps, often by night, through
the various parts of the country. The bigger the column, the easier
it is to obtain information about its projected movements, and it
may even prove possible to combine several parties together and
destroy it. If, however, the enemy's measures are so comprehensive
as to lead to unnecessary risk, it will often be better for the
guerillas to lie quiet for a month or so, or move to another district.

14. Conclusion: – All guerilla warfare and sabotage must be
directed towards lightning strokes against the enemy
simultaneously in widely distant areas, so as to compel him to
weaken his main forces by detaching additional troops to guard
against them. These strokes will frequently be most effective when
directed against his communications, thus holding up supplies and
eventually preventing him from undertaking large scale operations.
At the same time, however, action should be taken against
detachments, patrols, sentries, military lorries, etc., in such a way
that the whole country is made unsafe except for large columns
and convoys. This will hamper the enemy's plans effectively.

The civil population must be made to help by refusing to co-operate with the enemy, by providing information about the enemy, and by furnishing supplies and money to the guerillas. If they suffer inconvenience from your activities, either directly or as a result of enemy counter-measures, it must be explained to them that they are helping to defeat the enemy as much as their army at the front. The bolder the activities of the guerillas, and the greater the impunity with which they can act, owing to their careful planning and superior information, the more will the population despise the enemy, be convinced of his ultimate defeat, and help the guerillas.

Remember that you are fighting for your homeland, your mother, wife and children. Everything you can do to hamper and embarrass the enemy makes easier the task of your brothers-in-arms at the front who are fighting for you. As your activities develop, the enemy will become more and more ruthless in his attempts to stop you; the only effective reply to this is greater ruthlessness, greater courage, and an even wider development of your operations. Your slogan must be "Shoot, burn and destroy". **Remember that guerilla warfare is what a regular army has always most to dread. When this warfare is conducted by leaders of determination and courage, an effective campaign by your enemies becomes almost impossible.**

APPENDIX I. ROAD AMBUSH.

1. Planning.

(a) Find out by what roads small detachments and patrols of the enemy are accustomed to move. Select on one of these roads a locality which offers a good opportunity for ambushing.

2. Locality.

The following points should be looked for in selecting the locality for the ambush: –

(a) A line of retreat must be available which will give all the men a safe and sure way of escape. A thick wood, broken and rocky country, etc., give the best cover.

(b) Firing positions are required which enable fire to be opened at point-blank range. When there is no chance of prior discovery by the enemy, it may sometimes be of advantage to improve the position by building a stone or sandbag parapet. This should not be done, however, unless it can be concealed from aircraft.

(c) The locality should provide at least two fire positions and it is often better if these are on opposite sides of the road.

(d) It is best if the fire position enables the approaching enemy to be in view for three or four hundred yards. By this means it can be discovered in time if the enemy is in greater strength than expected; in such a case the enemy should be allowed to pass without being attacked.

3. Information.

Then get the following information: –

(a) Do the detachments move on foot, mounted, or in motor vehicles?

(b) What is the average strength of these detachments? How are they armed? How many vehicles?

(c) Do they use armoured cars and light tanks to patrol the roads?

(d) At what times do they pass the place you have chosen?

(e) Do they move in one block, or do they put men out in front and behind to guard against surprise? How do these men move, and how far from the main body?

(f) How will they try to summon assistance if attacked? Where is the nearest place such assistance can come from?

(g) If the detachment is carrying supplies, are those supplies of a type which can be easily destroyed by you, or be of use to you?

(h) What sort of troops are they, active or reserve, elderly, young, or what? Is there an officer with them? Can he be picked out and shot by the first volley? Can the N.C.O.s be picked out as well?

4. Action.

(a) The men must get into position without any chance of discovery. If there is any doubt, the position should be occupied by night.

(b) Sentries must be posted to give warning of the enemy's approach. They must be in sight of the firing position. It is not necessary to use guerillas for all sentry posts; a woman or child can sometimes be employed with advantage as they need not be in hiding.

(c) A simple system of signaling by sentries must be arranged. This can be the removal of a hat, doing up a shoelace or any natural action of that nature.

(d) If the enemy detachment is preceded by scouts, or a scouting vehicle, these should be allowed to pass on and not be fired at. Sometimes, however, it may be advantageous to place one or two guerillas further on from the firing position to shoot these scouts. **They must never be fired on, however, before the main attack begins; the guerilla leader must make certain this is known and understood.**

(e) The leader must give the signal to open fire. This can either be prearranged or given at the moment. Fire must be rapid fire, so as to have an immediate overwhelming effect.

(f) Two or three of the best shots must be detailed to shoot any officers or N.C.O.s. If these could not be recognized by their uniform, they can be discovered by noting who is shouting orders, etc.

(g) If the enemy appears to be destroyed, and it is intended to destroy or loot any cars or lorries, men for this task must be detailed beforehand. The rest must remain ready to open fire in case enemy are concealed in the lorries, or reinforcements arrive.

(h) The leader must give the signal to retire, and this signal must be unmistakable.

To judge the correct moment to break off the action is the leader's most difficult task. If the opening volleys of fire have not disorganized the enemy, it will probably be better to retire immediately, and be content with the damage done. If, however, the enemy detachment is completely destroyed, the opportunity should always be taken to seize all rifles, ammunitions, etc., and destroy or loot all other material. All papers and documents found should be taken away for examination. The dead must be searched for anything that may be useful.

(i) Remember that soldiers will always face the direction from which they are being fired at. It is usually best therefore to divide the party into two groups, on different sides of the road, of which only one group should fire first. The enemy will then face towards this group and start to attack and fire. The other group must then shoot the enemy in the back.

(j) **Sentries must remain in position until the leader gives the signal to fire.**

(k) Retirement when begun should be as rapid and dispersed as possible, i.e., the party must break up, and collect again as the leader may have ordered. Make full use of the time until the enemy hears of the attack to get right away from the scene.

(l) All wounded guerillas must be carried away if possible. It may be useful to have a few horses hidden at a short distance to carry wounded.

5. Road Blocks.

The use of road blocks by means of trenches, felled trees, rocks, etc., in conjunction with an ambush must be carefully considered.

At the commencement of guerilla warfare, before the enemy has had experience, it may be useful to have a block at the place of ambush, so as to force lorries to halt. When, however, the enemy is experienced, he will use scouts and patrols on all roads, and these will be warned by the blocks and so warn their N.C.O.s and drivers of vehicles immediately.

APPENDIX II. RAIL AMBUSH.

In general the rules for road ambushes apply to rail ambushes, so read them and make certain you understand them.

The difference between a rail ambush and a road ambush is that in a rail ambush you must combine some plan to wreck the train, either by derailing it, by blowing a mine under the engine, or other means. **It is not sufficient merely to shoot at the train; this would do more harm than good and must be avoided.**

(1) The principle is first to derail the train and then shoot down the survivors.

(2) Choose some place which is suitable for wrecking, for example, a high embankment where the falling engine will drag the coaches down with it; or a bridge, where the train will, with luck, fall into the river.

(3) Do **not** choose a place where trains run slowly; the faster the train is going, the better results you will get.

(4) The coaches at the rear of the train will probably suffer least damage; your first volleys should be directed against them.

(5) It is best to dispose your party in two groups, as in a road ambush, on opposite sides of the train.

(6) The signal to shoot will be when the wrecking starts or the mine is exploded. Everyone must start firing immediately.

(7) The train must not be looted until you are certain that all resistance by the enemy is at an end. After looting, it should be set on fire.

(8) If the train is armoured, and the wrecking has not been severe, it may be better to retire immediately. An armoured train will usually have many machine guns with it.

Read again the rules for a Road Ambush and apply them to this case.

Here are some methods of derailing a train: – To derail a train with certainty, both rails must be cut. This can be done very easily in the following ways: –

(1) One pound of high explosive pressed hard against the side of each rail.

(2) Three pounds of high explosive placed against the under side of each rail.

(3) Ten pounds of high explosive buried under the ballast not more than 4 inches from each rail.

(4) A single charge of fifty pounds of high explosive buried three or four feet deep between the rails. This will lift the locomotive ten feet into the air and is the best way where no bridge or steep slope can be found.

If the derailing is done by mehods (3) or (4), or where the ballast has been allowed to come close up under the rails by method (2) as well, it will be possible to lay the charge so that it will be undetected by day. Care must be taken not to show any signs of digging. A tin of water should be carried to wash down the stone ballast and clean it of earth adhering to it when using methods (3) or (4).

In all cases, it is best to fire the charge under or just in front of the front wheels of the locomotive. This can be done in two ways: –

(a) By means of an electric detonator with long wires leading to a battery where a man is concealed to operate it at the right moment.

(b) By means of a striker machine which is buried under a sleeper next to a rail joint. The weight of the locomotive passing over releases a striker which fires the charge by means of an instantaneous fuze.

In both cases, the detonator must be buried firmly in the explosive. When a battery is used, great care must be taken that the battery does not come near the ends of the wire till the last moment, to avoid accidents.

A length of wire up to 100 yards may be used leading away from the explosive to a hidden spot where it is fired.

Insulated wire such as is used for electric light in houses must be used. The accumulator battery out of a car is best but a good hand torch dry battery will do.

Diagrams of methods (1) and (2) of cutting rails: –

Method (1).

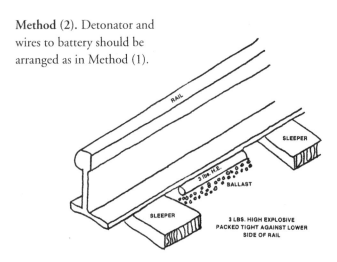

DETONATOR INSERTED IN EXPLOSIVE

PIECE OF WOOD TO ENSURE CHARGE IS TIGHT AGAINST RAIL

1 LB. H.E.

TWO WIRES FROM DETONATOR

STRING TYING ON THE CHARGE TO THE RAIL

Method (2). Detonator and wires to battery should be arranged as in Method (1).

RAIL

SLEEPER

3 lbs. H.E.

BALLAST

SLEEPER

3 LBS. HIGH EXPLOSIVE PACKED TIGHT AGAINST LOWER SIDE OF RAIL

Method of connecting electric detonators.

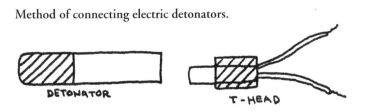

DETONATOR

T-HEAD

The electric detonator is in two parts: —

(1) The detonator, which is a small copper tube closed at one end and open at the other.

(2) The T head, which has two wires sticking out of one end and a very thin bridge of wire like the filament of a lamp the other. The filament end of the T head is pressed into the open end of the detonator. When an electric current passes through the filament it gets red hot and burns away completely but in doing so ignites the detonator. When wires are joined together or to the T head or battery, the covering must be cut away and the metal cleaned bright by scraping with a knife. The wires may then be twisted together. The bare wire at a joint must never touch anything, especially another joint. It is best to bind insulating tape or a piece of cloth round the joint. The joining of the wires for two charges fired by one battery is shown below.

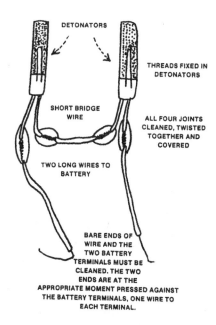

DETONATORS

THREADS FIXED IN DETONATORS

SHORT BRIDGE WIRE

ALL FOUR JOINTS CLEANED, TWISTED TOGETHER AND COVERED

TWO LONG WIRES TO BATTERY

BARE ENDS OF WIRE AND THE TWO BATTERY TERMINALS MUST BE CLEANED. THE TWO ENDS ARE AT THE APPROPRIATE MOMENT PRESSED AGAINST THE BATTERY TERMINALS, ONE WIRE TO EACH TERMINAL.

Destruction of Railway Engines: –

    (1) If you have no explosives, run off most of the water in the boiler and bank up the fire. The fire box, no longer cooled by the water, will get red hot and the steam pressure will bend it in.

    (2) If you have explosives, make it up into one pound packets each with a hand bomb time striker mechanism. This mechanism will explode the charge six seconds after the pin is pulled out. The best places to put these charges are on any of the large machined portions of the engine which the hand bombs will cover and are not more than 1" thick. If the engine is cold, open the smoke box in front and put a charge just inside one of the tube openings.

APPENDIX III. THE DESTRUCTION OF AN ENEMY POST, DETACHMENT OR GUARD.

    1. The object of this can be either to inflict casualties on the enemy, or to carry out the destruction of some place which the detachment is guarding.

    2. The detachment will usually be housed in a small house, hut, or tents, and will have taken steps to try and make these safe against attack. Remember, however, that if you use cunning, patience, and determination, no small post can be made impregnable and at the same time do its job of protection properly.

    3. Information:– You must get detailed information of the posts in your area, and then decide which offers the best chance of success. It may not be possible to get full details of all, but you will get enough information about some of them to enable you to select one and carry out a successful attack.

    4. The points on which you should get information are:

    (a) Strength of the detachment, number of officers, N.C.O.s etc.

(b) Who commands the detachment?

(c) Are the troops active or reserve? Are they old or young men? To what regiment or district do they belong?

(d) What arms and equipment do they carry? Have they machine guns?

(e) Is there a reserve of arms in the post? Where are they kept?

(f) What are the orders for safe custody of arms? Are any locked up?

(g) What means of communication has the post got – i.e.

   (i) Telegraph or telephone or wireless.

   (ii) Signal flags.

   (iii) Rockets.

   (iv) Pigeons.

   (v) Sirens, hooters.

   (vi) Messengers.

   ETC.

   Can any of these be destroyed when necessary?

(h) What sentries does the post provide –

   (i) On the railway, bridge, or store it is guarding?

   (ii) On the post itself?

(i) At what hours are sentries relieved –

   (i) By day?

   (ii) By night?

(k) How is relief carried out?

(l) Is there a group of men in the post always ready for immediate action? How strong is it?

(m) How long is each sentry's beat? What are its limits?

(n) What places can these sentries not see except by going to them?

(o) Are any civilians allowed to approach or enter the post, selling food, papers, etc.? Can you use any of these civilians to get information?

(p) Are there any searchlights in position?

(q) Is the post protected from barbed wire? Is this wire electrified? How do soldiers get in and out?

(r) Where does the post get its water supply from? Can the

source of water be destroyed?

(s) How often is the post and its guard inspected by someone from outside?

(t) How far away is the nearest re-inforcement, and how long would it take to come? Can it be ambushed on the way by another party?

(u) Can your destructive work be undertaken while the post is being fired at, or must the post first be destroyed completely.

(v) Can the post be blinded by smoke bombs for long enough to allow the destruction to be done?

(x) Are there watch-dogs, alarm traps, etc.?

ETC. ETC.

5. Plan: – This must depend on the information collected regarding the daily life and habits of the post, the state of alertness of the guard, its strength, armament, etc.

If the post is very small – say six to eight men – it may be possible to capture it by getting one or two men inside to seize the arms and hold up the guard at the moment the sentries are shot; on the other hand, it may be possible to rush the post from outside after shooting the sentries, to surround it and cut all communication, and shoot down all the men inside. It will also frequently be practicable to carry out destruction by one group while the other group of the party prevents the enemy of the post interfering. This depends to some extent on how long the destruction will take.

If the post is large, it will probably not be possible to destroy it. In such cases, if you wish to carry out some really important destructive work, it should be attempted by masking the post with heavy fire, smoke, etc. Such an attack has usually most chance of success when carried out by night.

In every case of an attack on a post, your first care must be to arrange for the destruction of means of communication – i.e., telegraph, wireless, etc. – unless you have a plan to ambush reinforcements.

Do not alarm any post that you mean eventually to attack – i.e., do not allow men to snipe it, to cut off its water supply, etc. Leave it absolutely quiet until the moment for attack comes. This will put the enemy off his guard.

APPENDIX IV. CONCEALMENT AND CARE OF ARMS AND EXPLOSIVES.

Try and get your arms before the enemy invades your country, so that you can conceal them more easily and at leisure.

1. One of the first acts of the enemy will be to demand the surrender of all arms held by the civil population.

2. All arms, bombs, etc., which are concealed must be protected against damp, rust, etc.; remember that your life and that of your friends may depend on a weapon in good order. The best way of preserving rifles, revolvers, etc., is to cover them with mineral jelly or vaseline, and wrap them in greasy paper or cloth.

They may then be safely buried.

3. Places where arms can be concealed are: –

(a) In the ground by burying. Choose a place where the earth has already been turned, or else go far away into a wood, etc.

(b) In the thatch or roof of a house.

(c) In a well-shaft, by making a chamber in the wall six feet or more down the shaft.

(d) In the banks of streams, in hollow trees, behind a waterfall, etc.

(e) In haystacks, potato or turnip heaps, ditches, culverts, etc.

(f) Do not use places like cellars, wooden floors, cattle sheds, etc., which the enemy is bound to search.

(g) As a last resort, give them to your women if caught unexpectedly.

4. You must make every effort to obtain arms and ammunition from the enemy during ambushes, raids, sniping, etc., as it will be difficult in time of war to replenish your stock by other means. Boxes of rifles and ammunition are frequently transported by rail and in lorries, inadequately guarded; find out when these are being carried and try and get them. Be very cautious of buying arms from a supposed enemy traitor. This is a common way of inducing you to walk into a trap.

APPENDIX V. THE ENEMYS INFORMATION SYSTEM AND HOW TO COUNTER IT.

As soon as guerilla warfare or sabotage commences, the enemy will set up an information organization in order to try and find out your organization, leaders and intentions. The methods he will employ are as follows: –

(1) Local agents, selected from amongst the inhabitants, and either bribed or compelled to act for him.

(2) Agents recruited from his own or other countries and imported into your area. These two types of agents can only be discovered by very careful work on your part, by getting information regarding arrivals of unknown people, by laying traps for suspected agents, etc.

(3) Special information branches that he will form.

(4) Captured prisoners and their interrogation.

(5) Captured documents which may reveal details of your organization, plans, names of partisans, etc. It is most important that no documents should be kept unless absolutely essential, and these should never be carried on the person for longer than necessary. This is usually the enemy's best source of information.

(6) Censorship of civilian letters.

(7) By placing agents among captured partisans. This is a difficult thing to counter and can only be met by strict discipline among the partisans in the prisons and concentration camps.

AMPHIBIAN, BREATHING APPARATUS

Catalogue No. N 258.

DESCRIPTION. This breathing apparatus consists of an oxygen bottle containing one and a half hours supply; also there is an automatic reducing device which ensures a flow of 1·5 to 2·0 litres per minute. The cannister of protosorb or carbon dioxide absorbent is connected to the breathing bag and purifies the exhaled air; a by-pass valve is also supplied if the flow does not prove sufficient.

METHOD OF USE. The main valve is turned on and a few puffs given on the by-pass, then the breathing bag is about two-thirds full. The mouthpiece is inserted, lungs emptied and valve opened. Breathing should be quite normal. If the breathing seems to be cut short, use the by-pass quite freely, in short quick puffs.

When the exhaust valve is beneath the surface, it must be opened.

***

WEIGHT. In air, 28¾ lbs. In water, 7½ lbs.

SHIPPING CLASSIFICATION.

Generic Title   -   -   Amphibian dual purpose breathing apparatus.

PACKING AND SPECIAL NOTES.

It should always be stowed dry and if possible, with a full cylinder of oxygen and empty protosorb canister, fitted as if for use.

It is most important to check all the valves, washers, etc., and the valves should be greased occasionally.

WEIGHT PACKED. 28¾ lbs.

PARACHUTIST, SUITS (STRIPTEASE SUITS)

Catalogue No. 22C/733 (Size 1). **22C/734** (Size 2)
22C/735 (Size 3). **22C/736** (Size 4).

GLOVES, GAUNTLET

GLOVES, LININGS, SILK

DESCRIPTION. These are made of either white or camouflaged canvas in four sizes. A zip fastener on each side is fitted for rapid exit from the suit, and these fasteners can be operated in either direction. A fly zip is also provided. On the left hip, is an external pocket for pistol and on the inside is a felt lined pocket designed to fit the spade, parachutist. Slightly to the rear of this pocket is a long narrow pocket for the spade handle.

At the lower outside edge of the left sleeve is a pocket for dagger or fighting knife and under each armpit, also outside, is a further pocket large enough to hold a second pistol, or emergency rations, etc. One large and one smaller pocket is fitted inside on the right.

A large pocket is provided to receive the spine pad, if used. This pocket is large enough to hold a brief case. At the neck is a leather strap to which is attached the helmet. All pockets have press stud fasteners.

The suits are large enough to permit of the wearing of two greatcoats if desired.

Flying Gauntlets with silk linings and Waistcoats, life saving, can also be used with these suits if required, in which case the standard R.A.F. pattern is provided.

DIMENSIONS.   **WEIGHT**

Size 1 - Up to 5 ft. 4 ins.
  ,, 2 - From 5 ft. 4 ins. to 5 ft. 8 ins.
  ,, 3 - From 5 ft. 8 ins. to 5 ft. 11 ins.   4½ lbs.
  ,, 4 - From 5 ft. 11 ins. to 6 ft. 4 ins.

PARACHUTISTS, HELMETS

Catalogue No. 22C/965 (Size 1). **22C/966** (Size 2). **22C/967** (Size 3). **22C/968** (Size 4).

DESCRIPTION. Made of similar material to the suits, parachutist and in the same colours. There are four sizes all fitted with mica goggles fastened to the back of the helmet. These goggles are trimmed with plush at the edges.

An adjustable soft leather chin strap is provided, and a strap at the base connects with that in the neck of the striptease suit.

The sides are extended to form ear flaps. Round the crown and over the skull, from front to rear, are ribs of padding to give protection to the wearer.

Press stud fittings are provided for oxygen mask and inter-communication microphone.
                                            WEIGHT 8 ozs.

WELROD, MK. II.A ('32)

Catalogue No. M 213.

DESCRIPTION. The Welrod is a firearm designed for silence. It is a compact tube weapon to be used in a two-handed grip, one hand gripping the magazine which acts as a pistol grip, and the other hand gripping the barrel of the silencer in a convenient forward position. The trigger action is similar to a colt automatic. Due to the high efficiency of the baffled silencer, a shot fired at 50 yards is not recognisable as a shot from a firearm.

The safety-catch is situated at the rear of the magazine housing, and is hand controlled. The sights are fixed and are sufficiently accurate to give 3 in. groups at up to 10 yards range. The recommended operational range is 8 yards.

METHOD OF USE. The magazine may be charged with one to five cartridges. The charged magazine is inserted into the housing, and the action is cocked by turning the breech operating handle in an anti-clockwise direction, and drawing the bolt to the rear. It is closed by driving the bolt home and turning the breech operating handle in a clockwise direction until it fully engages the stop.

DIMENSIONS. Mk. IIA. Overall length, 12¼".
9 mm. Overall length, 14⅜".

WEIGHT. 35 ozs.
3 lbs. 4 ozs.

PACKING AND SPECIAL NOTES.
As required.
Night sights on both types are a standard fitting.

ROPE, ALPINE

Catalogue No. K 167.

DESCRIPTION.

A fine manilla Rope, also containing either sisal or cord, having a breaking strain of 22 cwt.

For use as a knotted climbing rope or for making up into rope ladders.

DIMENSIONS. Circumference 1½"

WEIGHT. 7¾ lbs. per 100 ft.

PACKING AND SPECIAL NOTES.
As required.
Usually supplied in 120 ft. lengths.

Catalogue No. K 168.

ROPE, LADDERS

DESCRIPTION. Rope Ladders or Knotted Climbing Ropes are made to any desired specification. The Rope can be of any thickness, but Rope, Alpine (Item No. 167) is recommended.

A Standard Rope Ladder 9" wide has 19 rungs, each 9" apart and is fitted with a Grapnel.

DIMENSIONS. 16½" long.   **WEIGHT.** 11½ lbs.

PACKING AND SPECIAL NOTES. As required.

Catalogue No. N 298.

PAPER, NITRATED

DESCRIPTION. This paper is similar to and as strong as air mail paper, the sheets having a red edge. It may be used for writing, printing, typing or duplicating and can be destroyed by fire faster than similar ordinary paper and is normal in appearance. Although it absorbs ink freely, the writing will still remain legible.

METHOD OF USE. To destroy it, apply flame or spark to a point on the paper; this may be done through a small hole in the envelope or wrapper.

DIMENSIONS. Single sheet 10" x 7½"

SHIPPING CLASSIFICATION.
Generic Title · · Nitrocellulose.
Explosive Group · III.
Storage and Stowage · II. M.S.B.

PACKING AND SPECIAL NOTES. As required. Do not file with ordinary paper. The paper should be stored under reasonably dry conditions with not more than 20 sheets in one pack. Limited supplies available.

TYREBURSTER

DESCRIPTION. It consists of an outer case of thin tinned steel in two overlapping and loosely fitted halves, containing a ring of H.E., in the centre of which is a special pressure switch. A minimum load of 150 lbs. on the case causes the two halves to telescope and the mechanism to operate and set off the charge.

METHOD OF USE. The Tyreburster is placed on the road or in ground where vehicles are likely to move. On soft ground a stone or other hard body should be placed under the Tyreburster. If this is not done the device may be pushed into the ground by the vehicle without exploding.

DIMENSIONS. Diam. 5 cms. Thickness 2 cms.　　　　　**WEIGHT.** 4 ozs.

SHIPPING CLASSIFICATION.　Generic Title　-　-　Destructors Contact.

　　　　　　　　　　　　　　　　Explosive Group　-　VI.

　　　　　　　　　　　　　　　　Storage and Stowage　　O.A.S.

PACKING AND SPECIAL NOTES.

　　Camouflaged and packed as required.

　　Camouflaged Bursters representing a wide variety of rocks are already in production.

SWITCH NO. 10
(TIME PENCILS)

Catalogue No. A I.

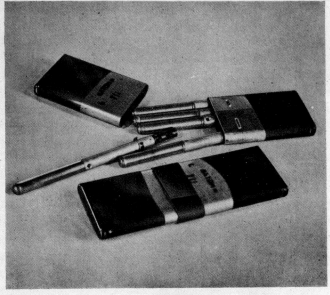

DESCRIPTION. This is a delay action fuze-shaped liked a pencil. One end consists of a copper tube, the other end is a spring snout which will take a No. 8 Detonator or a length of Bickford. Timings vary between 10 minutes and 24 hours and are indicated by colours shown on the safety strip of the switch. The copper tube can be crushed by hand and this breaks a glass ampoule inside containing a corrosive liquid. This liquid attacks a steel wire restraining a spring loaded striker. When the corrosion is complete the striker is released to fire a cap which ignites a safety fuze or detonator.

METHOD OF USE.

(1) Insert the detonator or safety fuze in the spring snout.

(2) Crush the ampoule containing the liquid, by squeezing the copper tube.

(3) Shake the pencil to ensure that the liquid is in good contact with the steel wire.

(4) Remove the safety strip.

DIMENSIONS. 5¼" long x ⅜" diameter.   **WEIGHT.** 0.65 ozs.

SHIPPING CLASSIFICATION. Generic Title   -   Igniter, Fuze.
Explosive Group   -   VI.
Storage and Stowage   -   I.   O.A.S.

PACKING AND SPECIAL NOTES.   **DIMENSIONS.**   **WEIGHT.**
5 Switches per tin - 5⅝" x 1⅞" x ⅞"   5 ozs.
150 Tins per case :   16¾" x 13" x 7¾"   62 lbs.

TIMINGS. The period of delay for the switch is indicated by the colour of the Safety Strip. The timings given below are for 15°C. but at higher temperatures the delays are considerably shortened.

Black, 10 mins.   Red, ½ hr.   White, 2 hrs.
Green, 5½ hrs.   Yellow, 12 hrs.   Blue, 24 hrs.

HAVERSACKS, GUERILLA

Catalogue No. N 253.

DESCRIPTION.

Webbing Haversack, can be worn on the back or slung at the side. It has two loops for a belt for support, when worn at the side.

It carries one Sten Gun, and has pockets for seven loaded magazines, four hand grenades and detonators. There is also room for any personal equipment.

DIMENSIONS. 14" x 3¾"

PACKING AND SPECIAL NOTES.
As required.

PACKS, QUICK RELEASE

Catalogue No. J 224.

DESCRIPTION. The Pack comprises two main assembles; the Cradle and the Bag or Pack. The cradle is a wooden frame curved to fit the back, to which is attached a head strap, the shoulder straps and the Quick Release Buckle.

The Pack consists of a large Bag having two pockets, which will hold approximately one hundred pounds in weight. The Pack is attached to the Cradle by eye-screws supplied on the right and left hand sides of the Cradle Frame.

METHOD OF USE. The operator must grasp the release cord firmly in his left hand at the lowest point and exert a sharp downward pull, at the same time jerking off the head band.

DIMENSIONS. 24" deep. 18" wide. 3" thick.　　　**WEIGHT.** 6 lbs. (average).

PACKING AND SPECIAL NOTES. As required.

MONEY BELT, SUEDE

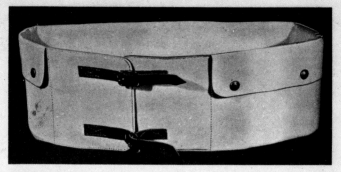

DESCRIPTION.

Type 1. 6″ deep. Length of pockets vary according to waist measurements. Three pockets with zip fasteners.

Type 2. 4½″ deep. Length of pockets vary according to waist measurements. Three pockets with press-button fastenings.

PACKING AND SPECIAL NOTES.

As required.

This is not a special store, but belts are made up to personal dimensions, etc., when requested.

MUCUNA
(ITCHING POWDER)

Catalogue No.
NS 300.

DESCRIPTION. This powder is composed of minute seed hairs which owing to their peculiar structure cause considerable itching when applied to the skin.

METHOD OF USE. The greatest effect is produced by applying the powder to the inside of underclothing.

PACKING AND SPECIAL NOTES.

As required.

This material is supplied in foot powder tins for the purpose of camouflage.

They should be trained never to talk about their military matters, to mention names, or to give away any information at all. Steps must be taken within prisons by the partisans to test and try out every prisoner who comes in, to make absolutely certain that he is not an agent in disguise.

(8) **Listening sets:** – These will also be placed in prisons and camps, so all conversation must be restricted to general matters and nothing said which might lead to the capture or death of your compatriots.

(9) Men who are captured must at once organize themselves in the prison to censor all their own letters that they are writing to friends outside, and to censor all incoming letters to individual prisoners.

(10) The best method of dealing with informers is their ruthless extermination when discovered, as described in the main part of this book.

(11) Prisoners who are being interrogated may be tempted by the fact that there is only one enemy in the room to give away information if pressed, as they may feel that only one person will know it. All men must know that this is not correct; not only will the enemy install listening sets in the room in which the prisoners are interrogated in order that two or three people may hear any confession, but also all the information a prisoner gives, and his name and district, will be taken down in writing and distributed everywhere. His comrades would then eventually discover his treachery and he would be dealt with suitably when the enemy has been defeated.

You must try and break up or hinder the enemy's information organization by all means. The most effective is the destruction of the personnel engaged on that work. Intelligence officers, N.C.O.s, etc., will frequently work individually and move about the countryside. Opportunities must be sought to kill them and destroy or carry off any papers they are carrying.

APPENDIX VI. HOW TO COUNTER ENEMY ACTION.

The enemy will make use of his superior armament to try and break up guerilla activities. Here are some of the methods he will employ, and ways for you to counter them.

(1) **Aeroplanes:** – These will be used to search the country for guerilla parties, and possibly also to attack them. The best counter is concealment, therefore move as much as you can by night. By day, on the approach of an aeroplane, men must be taught to get under whatever cover is available, **and to lie still with faces to the ground.** Movement and human faces show up to aeroplanes at once.

Do not fire at an aeroplane unless actually attacked by it. Remember that an aeroplane, if it sees you, will at once report your position to the nearest military detachment who will come out after you. Therefore, if you think your party has been seen, move off at once to some other place, and keep a good look-out.

(2) **Tanks, armoured cars, armour-plated lorries etc.:** – Do not shoot at these haphazardly, it will have no effect unless you have anti-tank rifles and bombs, etc. You must lay a proper trap if you are trying to destroy them – i.e. a road mine or block, or the vehicle must be halted. Remember that these vehicles shut down their windows when attacked, and are then very blind; it will then be possible for bold men to crawl close enough to bomb them or set them on fire with petrol.

(3) **Gas:** – The enemy will only use gas if he gets you in a corner and other methods fail. Therefore your first precaution must be to avoid being caught where you cannot get away. Your information of the enemy's plans and proper posting of sentries and look-outs when the party is collected will prevent you being caught. If you hear that the enemy intends using gas against guerillas, all men should provide themselves with gas-masks.

(4) **Shells, bombs, grenades:** – Against these weapons the best

protection is to be down flat behind any cover available, such as a bank, ditch, etc.

(5) **Machine-guns, etc.:** – Smoke bombs can be used to create a smoke screen between yourself and the machine-gun so as to enable you to get away.

APPENDIX VII. GUERILLA INFORMATION SERVICE.

1. Early information of the enemy's moves, strength, intention, etc., is vitally important. You must therefore impress on all your compatriots the necessity of passing on to some members of the party any information they hear. The following, owing to their occupations, are in a good position to get news: –

(a) Innkeepers, hawkers.

(b) Waitresses, barmaids, etc.

(c) Postmen, telephone and telegraph operators.

(d) Station-masters, railway porters and staffs.

(e) Doctors, priests, dentists, hospital staff.

(f) Domestic servants, barbers.

(g) Shopkeepers, newsagents.

(h) Contractors, camp followers, camp sanitary men.

(i) All people who have access to military camps, establishments, etc.

(j) Discontented enemy soldiers.

2. Domestic servants and cafe attendants are particularly valuable agents; they must be encouraged to gain the confidence of the enemy soldiers, and be on easy and intimate terms with them. Suitable agents of this type should be introduced into houses where enemy officers are billeted, etc. It is a natural weakness of soldiers in a hostile country to react favourably to acts of courtesy and kindness from women; such men will frequently drop unsuspecting hints that they are shortly going on patrol, etc. The agent must then find out as much detail as possible and pass it on at once.

3. Discontented soldiers must be discovered, i.e., those who have recently been punished, have had their pay stopped, etc. These, if encouraged, may give useful information.

4. Information should be passed by word of mouth unless that is impossible. If impossible, it must be written and sent by messenger (children frequently make good messengers) or placed in a pre-arranged place, and then destroyed by the recipient.

APPENDIX VIII. SABOTAGE METHODS.

Sabotage means any act done by individuals that interferes with the enemy and so helps your people to defeat him. It covers anything from the shooting of a sentry to the blowing-up of an ammunition dump. The following are various acts, and the best of way of carrying out the difficult ones: –

(1) **Lorries, cars, tanks, etc.:** – Burn them by knocking a hole in the bottom of the petrol tank, and setting fire to the escaping petrol. If you can't burn them, put water or sugar in the petrol tank, or remove the magneto, etc. – This will temporarily disable the vehicle.

(2) **Munition Dumps:** – The best method is to lay a charge of explosive among the shells and then explode it, but it will be rare that you will get an opportunity to do this unless you are disguised as an enemy soldier. There are other ways. If the dump is in a building, a good way is to set fire to the building, Use oil-soaked rags, shavings, thermite bomb. If the dump is in an open field or by the road, throw a special bomb into it (this must be a bomb with at least one kilogramme of explosive in it, and you must hit a shell or it will not be effective).

(3) **Cement:** – Open the sacks, and pour water on them, or leave them for rain and moisture to get in.

(4) **Hay, Forage:** – Burn or throw acid or disinfectant.

(5) **Petrol stocks:** – Use a special bomb or thermite bomb.

(6) **Refrigerator sheds, and refrigerator railway vans:** – Destroy the refrigerating apparatus.

(7) Sniping and killing sentries, stragglers, etc. Get a rifle or revolver with a silencer, but use a knife or noose when you can. This has a great frightening effect. Don't act unless you are certain you can get away safely. Nighttime is best and has the best effect on enemy nerves. Get used to moving about in the dark yourself. Wear rubber shoes and darken your face.

(8) **Telegraph lines on roads and railways:** – Cut these whenever possible. When you cannot reach them, throw over a rope with a weight on the end and try and drag them down. Cut down a tree so that it will fall across them.

(9) **Railways:** – Jam the points by hammering a wooden wedge into them. Cut signal wires. Set fire to any coaches and wagons you can get at. If you can use explosive, try and destroy the points. Remember that railways can carry very little traffic if the signalling apparatus is intefered with, and this traffic must go very slowly.

(10) **Water Supplies:** – Contaminate water which is used by the enemy. Use paraffin, strong disinfectants, salt, etc.

(11) Destruction of leading marks, buoys, lightships, etc., in navigable waters.

(12) **Burning of soldiers' cinemas, theatres:** – Cinema films are highly inflammable. The cinema should be fired **during a performance** by firing the films in the operator's box. This should easily be arranged.

(13) Time bombs, eigar-shaped, are very suitable for placing in trains, lorries, etc. They are made of lead tubing, divided into two halves by a copper disc. Suitable acids are put in each half, and when they have eaten the copper away, the acids combine and form an intensely hot flame, which will set fire to anything with which it comes into contact. The thickness of the copper disc determines when the bomb will go off. Get some of these bombs.

ALL IN FIGHTING, 1942
SOE

REPRINTED AS GET TOUGH, 1943
OSS

Captain W. E. Fairbairn's *All-In Fighting*, later published in the US as *Get Tough*, is probably the best-known unarmed- and knife-combat manual of the period. But it was certainly not the only one: others available at the time included Bernard's *Manual of Commando and Guerilla Warfare* and the Ju-Jitsu based James Hipkiss manual *Unarmed Combat*. Before the war Fairbairn was self-defence instructor with the Shanghai Police, and from 1940 was employed in the UK. Together with Captain E. Sykes, he designed the Fairbairn-Sykes combat knife, which was used by the Commandos as well as clandestine forces, and also produced the booklet *Shooting to Live* (1942) and a self-defence manual for women. At Arisaig in Scotland, Fairbairn and Sykes taught SOE trainees both advanced pistol techniques and close combat, and later this was extended to OSS at Camp X in Canada with the assistance of Colonel Rex Applegate. Colonel Applegate would promulgate similar ideas in the US with his book *Kill or Get Killed*.

Knife combat has rightly been described as a messy business. Agents were taught throat and artery slashing, thrusts to vital areas, and how to avoid difficult targets such as thickly padded coats. When a kill had to be unobtrusive, the attacker's jacket was removed first, then replaced over the inevitable blood stains on his clothes. If there was a significant problem with the use of fighting knives it was that they were a clear indicator of Allied involvement in an operation. In Yank Levy's *Guerilla Warfare*, the improvised use of hammers, sandbags, hat pins, and bags of coins were all recommended, because they would not readily be recognised as weapons and blow the cover of the user. Smaller knives and 'bodkins' were also designed to be hidden up sleeves, inside pencils, inside clothing and under lapels.

In the following pages we show a selection of the many techniques demonstrated in Fairbairn's manual.

BLOWS
No. I. Edge of the Hand

Edge of the hand blows are delivered with the inner (i.e. little finger) edge of the hand, fingers straight and thumb extended; the actual blow being made with the edge only, about half way between the knuckle of the little finger and the wrist, as shown in Fig. 1.

1. The blow is delivered from a bent arm (never with a straight arm), using a chopping action from the elbow, with the weight of the body behind it. Students are advised to practise this blow by striking the open palm of their left hand, as in Fig. 2.

2. There are two ways in which this blow can be delivered:
(a) **downwards,** with either hand;
(b) **across,** with either hand; the blow always being delivered outwards, with the palm of the hand downward, never on top (Fig. 3).

The following are the points on your opponent's body that should be attacked, every blow being delivered as quickly as possible.

(a) on the sides or back of the wrist;
(b) on the forearm, half way between the wrist and elbow;
(c) on the biceps;
(d) on the sides or back of the neck;
(e) just below the 'Adam's apple';
(f) on the kidney or base of the spine.

Note:– In the event of your opponent having caught hold of you, strike his wrist or forearm; a fracture will most likely result. This would be almost impossible with a blow from a clenched fist.

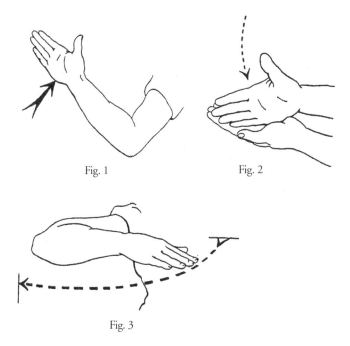

Fig. 1

Fig. 2

Fig. 3

No. 2. Chin Jab

The chin jab is delivered with the heel of the hand, full force and with the weight of the body behind it, fingers spread so as to reach the eyes, as in Fig. 4: the point aimed at is your opponent's chin (Fig. 5).

1. The blow is delivered upwards from a bent arm and only when close to your opponent. The distance the blow will have to travel will depend on the height of your opponent, but it will seldom exceed six inches.

2. The hand must never be drawn back, 'signalling' the intention of striking. From start to finish, every movement must be made as quickly as possible.

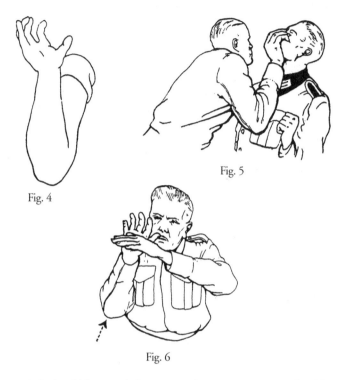

Fig. 4

Fig. 5

Fig. 6

3. It should be noted that an attack or attempt to attack with the knee at your opponent's testicles will always bring his chin forward and down.

Note.– Students should practise this blow as follows: hold your left hand at the height of your own chin, palm downwards; jab up quickly with your right, striking your left hand as in Fig. 6.

No. 3. Boot (Side Kick)

With a few exceptions, the kick with the boot should be made sideways. It will be noted that in this method you are able to put more force behind your blow and can, if necessary, reach farther.

1. Turn sideways to your opponent, taking the weight of your body on your left foot. Bending your left leg slightly from your knee, raise your right foot two to four inches off the ground, as in Fig. 7. Shoot your right foot outwards to your right, aiming to strike your opponent's leg just below the knee-cap.

2. Follow the blow through, scraping your opponent's shin with the edge of the boot from the knee to the instep, finishing up with all your weight on your right foot, and smash the small bones of the foot, if necessary, follow up with a chin jab with your left hand (Fig. 8).

Note.– Where the kick is to be made with the left foot, reverse the above.

Fig. 7   Fig. 8

No. 3(a). Boot Defence

Your opponent has seized you around the waist from in front, pinning your arms to your sides.

1. Having taken your weight on one foot, raise the other and scrape your opponent's shin bone downwards from about half-way from the knee, finishing up with a smashing blow on his foot (Fig. 9).

2. An alternative method to Fig, 9, permitting you to use the inner edge of the boot, should be applied as in Fig. 10.

Note A.– The question of when you should use the outside or inside of your boot will depend upon how the weight of your body is distributed at the time. Provided that you are equally balanced on both feet, you can use either; otherwise, use the opposite one to that on which you have your weight.

Note B.– If seized from behind, stamp on your opponent's foot with the heel of either boot, turning quickly, and follow up with a chin jab with either hand.

Fig. 9

Fig. 10

No. 3 (b). Boot. 'Bronco Kick'

It is not advisable to attempt to kick your opponent with the toe of your boot when he is lying on the ground, unless you have hold of an arm or clothing, etc. Method recommended:

1. Take a flying jump at him, drawing your feet up by bending your knees, at the same time keeping your feet close together (Fig. 11).

2. When your feet are approximately eight inches above your opponent's body, shoot your legs out straight, driving both of your boots into his body, and smash him.

Note.– It is almost impossible for your opponent to parry a kick made in this manner, and in addition it immediately puts him on the defensive, leaving him only one alternative of rolling away from you in an attempt to escape. Further, it should be noted that although he may attempt to protect his body with his arms, he cannot prevent you from killing him. The reason for this is that the sharp edges of the iron heel-plates of your boots, which cover a surface of much less than half an inch, are driven into your opponent's body by the combined strength of your legs, each delivering a blow of approximately 75 lb. = 150 lb., plus the weight of your body, say – 150 lb.: Total 300 lb.

Now try to visualize a peg of approximately half an inch being struck with a 300-lb. force and how far it would be driven into a man's body; or better still practise the kick on a dummy figure or on the grass as in Fig. 12.

Fig. 11

Fig. 12

No. 4. Knee

It will be noted that this blow can only be delivered when you are very close to your opponent.

1. Taking the weight of your body on one leg, bend the knee of the other by drawing your heel slightly backwards, and drive your knee quickly upwards into your opponent's fork, as in Fig. 13.

Note.– In addition to being a method of attack and defence, it is frequently used for the purpose of bringing your opponent in a more favourable position for applying the chin jab (Fig. 14).

Fig. 13

Fig. 14

No. 6 (a). Strangle (Two Hands)

You are seized by the throat as in Fig. 23.

1. Seize your opponent's right elbow with your left hand from underneath, your thumb to the right.

2. Reach over his arms and seize his right wrist with your right hand (Fig. 24).

3. Apply pressure on his left arm with your right, at the same time with a circular upward motion of your left hand, force his elbow towards your right side. This will break his hold of your throat and put him off balance (Fig. 25).

4. Keeping a firm grip with both hands, turn rapidly towards your right-hand side by bringing your right leg to your right rear. Follow up with edge of hand blow on his elbow (Fig. 26).

Note.– All the above movements must be continuous.

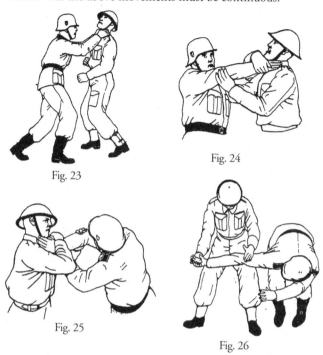

Fig. 23

Fig. 24

Fig. 25

Fig. 26

No. 7(a). Bear Hug (Front, over the Arms)

(An alternative method to No. 7 [not included here].)
You are gripped around the waist.

1. If possible, bite his ear. Even although not successful, this will cause him to bend forward and into a position from which you can seize his testicles with your right hand (Fig. 28.

2. Reach over his arm with your left forearm (Fig. 29).

3. Apply pressure on his right arm with your left (causing him to

break his hold) and force his head downwards. Smash him in the face with your right knee (Fig. 30).

If necessary, follow up with edge of hand blow on back of his neck.

Note.– Should your opponent anticipate your intention when you are in the position shown in Fig. 29 and resist the pressure of your left arm (para. 3), go after his eyes with your left hand as in Fig. 30A [not shown here], and follow up with a knee to the testicles.

Fig. 28

Fig. 29

Fig. 30

Fig. 31

No. 9 (a). Bear Hug (Back, over the Arms)

(An alternative method to No. 9 [not included here].)
You are gripped around the waist.

1. Seize his testicles with your left hand (causing him to break his hold).

2. Pass your right arm over his right, as in Fig. 34.

3. Slip out from under his arm by turning to your left and stepping backwards with your right foot, seizing his right wrist with both hands and jerking it downwards. Finish up by kicking him in the face, as in Fig. 35.

No. 10. Bear Hug (Back, Arms Free)

You are gripped around the waist as in Fig. 36.

1. Smash him in the face with your tin hat.

2. Stamp on his feet with either foot.

3. Seize his little finger with your right hand, bend it backwards, and walk out of the hold, as in Fig. 37.

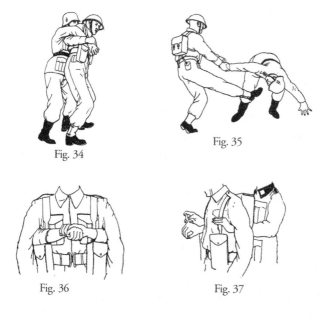

Fig. 34

Fig. 35

Fig. 36

Fig. 37

No. 21. Chair

Most lion-tamers consider a small chair to be sufficient to keep a lion from attacking them. Should you be so fortunate as to have a chair handy when your opponent is attacking you with a knife, seize the chair as in Fig. 72. Rush at him, jabbing one or more of the legs of the chair into his body. The odds in favour of your overpowering your opponent are roughly three to one, and well worth taking (Fig. 73).

Fig. 72

Fig. 73

No. 22. The Match-Box Attack

You are sitting down, say, in a railway carriage, or have picked up a hitch-hiker. Your opponent, who is on your left, sticks a gun in your ribs, holding it in his right hand.

1. Take a match-box and hold it as in Fig. 74, the top of the box being slightly below the finger and thumb.

2. Keeping the upper part of the right arm close to the right side of your body, with a circular upward motion of your right fist, turning your body from the hip, strike your opponent hard on the left side of his face, as near to the jaw-bone as possible (Fig. 75); parry the gun away from your body with your left forearm.

Note.– The odds of knocking your opponent unconscious by this method are at least two to one. The fact that this can be accomplished with a match-box is not well-known, and for this reason is not likely to raise your opponent's suspicion of your movements. Naturally, all movements, from the initial start of the blow, must be carried out with the quickest possible speed.

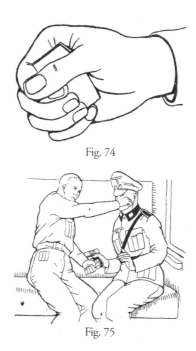

Fig. 74

Fig. 75

No. 23. Smacking the Ears

This method should be applied when your opponent has no protection over his ears:

1. Cup your hands, keeping the fingers and thumb bent, and close together, as in Fig. 76.

2. Strike your opponent simultaneously over both ears, using five to ten pounds force with both hands, Fig. 77.

Note.– This will probably burst one or both ear-drums and at least give him a mild form of concussion, and make him what is known in boxing circles as punch-drunk. You will then have no difficulty in dealing with him in any way you may wish.

So that students may realize what the effect of a blow given as above is like, we recommend that they should apply it on themselves, as in Fig. 41. Care must be taken to use *only* half a pound force with each hand.

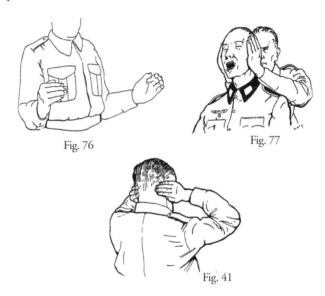

Fig. 76

Fig. 77

Fig. 41

No. 25. Attack with a Small Stick or Cane *(contd.)*

You are close up and facing your opponent, as in Fig. 88.

1. Strike your opponent *across* the stomach with the left end of the stick by a vicious circular motion towards your right-hand side.

In delivering this blow, there are four essential points that must be carried out simultaneously:

(a) Your loose grip on the stick, both hands, must be changed to as strong as possible.

(b) The movement of your left hand is towards your right-hand side.

(c) The movement of your right hand is inwards to the left, but much shorter than that of the left hand, owing to your right hand coming against your right side.

(d) The movement of your left foot is forward towards the right. This permits you to put the weight of your body behind the blow. See Fig. 89.

Note.– This blow *across* your opponent's stomach would not, if he was wearing thick clothing, put him 'out', but it will surely make him bring his chin forward, which is exactly the position you want him in:

2. Keeping the firmest possible grip of the stick with both hands, jab upwards with the end of the stick (left-hand end) and drive it into his neck and kill him (Fig. 90), The mark you are after is that soft spot about two inches back from the point of the chin.

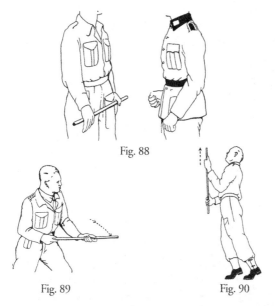

Fig. 88

Fig. 89

Fig. 90

You have missed your opponent's chin when you attacked as in Fig. 90:

3. Smash him down the face with the end of the stick, as in Fig. 91, putting all the weight of the body behind the blow.

4. If necessary, follow-up with a smash across the left side of your opponent's face with the right-hand end of the stick, as in Fig. 92.

Note.– You have taken a step to your left front with your right foot to permit of the weight of the body being behind the blow.

5. If at any time, after the initial attack across the stomach, your opponent's head is high in the air, exposing the front part of his neck, aim to strike the Adam's apple with the centre of the stick, putting every ounce of strength behind the blow. This should kill him, or at least knock him unconscious (Fig. 93).

Note.– Methods No. 2 (the point, up under the chin) and No. 5 (the centre, into the Adam's apple) are finishing-off or killing blows, but you must first bring your opponent into the position that permits you to deal them effectively. Method No. 1 (the point across the stomach) will, on account of its unexpectedness, enable you to accomplish this, and your attack should always start with the stomach attack.

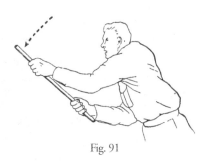

Fig. 91

Fig. 92

Fig. 93

DISARMING
No. 30. Disarm, from in Front

You are held-up with a pistol and ordered to put your hands up. The fact that you have not been shot on sight clearly shows that your opponent wants to take you as a prisoner or is afraid to fire, knowing that it will raise an alarm.

Lead him to suppose, by your actions, etc., that you are scared to death, and wait until such time as he is close up to you. Providing all your movements are carried out with speed, it is possible for you to disarm him, with at least a ten to one chance of success.

1. Hold your hands and arms as in Fig. 127.

2. With a swinging downward blow of your right hand, seize your opponent's right wrist, simultaneously turning your body sideway towards the left. This will knock the pistol clear of your body (Fig. 128). Note that the thumb of your right hand is on top.

3. Seize the pistol with the left hand as in Fig. 129.

4. Keeping a firm grip with the right hand on his wrist, force the pistol backwards with your left hand, and knee him or kick him in the testicles (Fig. 130).

Note.– All the above movements must be continuous.

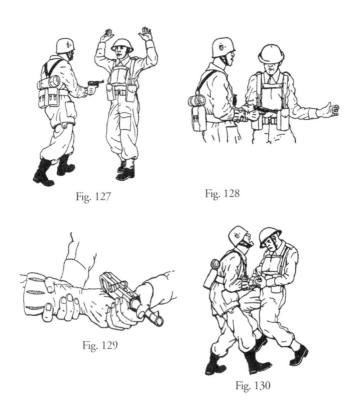

Fig. 127

Fig. 128

Fig. 129

Fig. 130

PROPAGANDA EFFORTS
AGAINST HITLER

FROM THE SOE AND OSS FILES,
1941–1944

As is clear from the internal OSS documents reprinted here the effort to undermine the 'cult of the Führer' and make Hitler appear ridiculous to the German people was one of the most bizarre episodes in the history of secret warfare. One of its key triggers was a lengthy document by Walter C. Langer of the Morale Operations section, entitled *A Psychological Analysis of Adolf Hitler, his Life and Legend*. This attempted to help 'frame a counter propaganda' in the light of Hitler's psychological and personality characteristics such as his belief in destiny, lack of emotional control, odd sexual preferences and general rejection of intellectuals. OSS was certainly not alone in applying these approaches. Stalin was always interested in the psychology of Hitler, and even at the end of the war went to considerable trouble to have a comprehensive dossier composed on his rival's personal history.

The use of tame astrologers to predict dire consequences for the Germans and pseudo-mystic cranks to expose the supposed credulous beliefs of Nazi leaders was pioneered by the British. In May 1941 SOE sent astrologer Ludwig von Wohl to the US where his mission was to disseminate predictions inimical to the German war effort. In 1942 the Political Warfare Executive followed up with a black propaganda booklet in German, which planted the ideas that Hitler was taking hormones, was under the malign influence of his physician, and that he had made his own astrologer 'disappear' when he became displeased with him.

The concrete effects of these early and somewhat fantastical essays in psychological operations were negligible. It is interesting to note, however, that at least some of the content was picked up in Allied nations where, paradoxically, speculation on Hitler's mental and physical health, sexual proclivities, and credulity towards mumbo-jumbo appears to have been something of a morale raiser.

Allied secret propagandists made a very late start when it is considered that Nazi book banning, state-sponsored film, postcards, newspapers, party rallies and posters were all well established in Germany by the mid-1930s. The first responses to such German efforts were pedestrian and uninspired but, as can be seen from the examples at the end of this chapter, significant strides, and much increased realism were achieved by the middle of the war.

Office of Strategic Services

Interoffice Memo

TO: MCPC Committee   DATE: August 3, 1943

FROM: Eugene P. Harper

SUBJECT: Hitler Taking Dancing Lessons

This will be a series of picture postcards, to be kept in a deck, like a deck of cards.

1. Show a fake news clipping in German stating that because of war strain Hitler's doctor has ordered more exercise and der Fuhrer has decided on dancing as the most practical exercise.

2. Faked picture of Hitler being instructed in folk dance by a male teacher. Both are smiling coyly.

3. Faked pictures of Hitler dancing with children.

4. Faked picture of Hitler dancing with a fat frau. He is kicking up his heels in wild abandon and laughing joyously.

5. Faked picture of Hitler doing dance in his office. German generals stand in background scowling.

6. Faked picture of Hitler dancing in Goebbels' back yard. Goebbels' children applauding. Goebbels frowns. (A newsphoto recently appeared of Goebbels' children.)

7. Faked picture of Hitler in male ballet costume in exotic pose.

OFFICE OF STRATEGIC SERVICES
WASHING D.C.

DATE: September 6, 1943

TO: Lt. Dolan
      Mr. Cushing

FROM: Lt. D. V. McGranahan

SUBJECT: "Heel" Campaign

Here is the revised edition of the anti-Hitler ("Heel") campaign. What next?

CAMPAIGN AGAINST HITLER

It has been agreed by the various German experts of OSS that the time is now ripe for an intensive MO campaign against Hitler. The aim of the campaign is to undermine German respect for Hitler and to widen the cleavage between him and other power elements in Germany.

To achieve this goal, certain main lines of attack have been decided upon. These lines of attack follow, and under each is listed a series of implementing ideas. MO will undertake to spread these ideas through rumors and through other concrete operations suggested in the appendix [not shown here].

1. <u>To destroy the Hitler myth and bring der Führer down to the level of an ordinary party leader.</u> To do this we must stress the human failings and foibles of der Führer.

<u>Suggested Implementation:</u>

a. In spite of the great paper shortage, Hitler has refused to eliminate compulsory purchases of Mein Kampf by newly married couples, etc. Hitler prefers to keep his 40% royalties, war or no war.

b. Hitler personally profited at the rate of 1 RM for every kilometer of road built in Germany during the 30's.

c. The available paper supply and printing facilities in Germany have been increasingly absorbed by Mein Kampf and other Party publications. Hitler and the Party leaders have thus succeeded in maintaining their private incomes from these sources, although German students must do without textbooks, and great newspapers like the Frankfurter Zeitung must be suspended.

d. Hitler is terrified by air-raids and has, therefore, never visited an area which has just been bombed and is apt to be bombed again.

e. Hitler rejects pleas from Goebbels that he visit areas devastated by Allied raids. He does not have the courage to face the people.

f. A Parisian connoisseur, after seeing Hitler's collection of pornographic pictures, stated that it was the best in Europe.

g. Hitler has a special plane bringing him asparagus and bon-bons fresh daily from Paris.

h. Hitler now has five luxurious country estates which he visits in rotation so that he will not appear to be spending too much time in any one of them.

i. Hitler has refused to confer with his generals since the time they upbraided him for his Wagnerian conception of military strategy. He issues grandiose commands from his private headquarters, but the generals pay little attention to them.

2. To picture Hitler as utterly unsympathetic toward the loss of life and the suffering of the individual German.

Suggested Implementation:

a. Hitler has declared, "I will not stop fighting until 10,000,000 Germans have died." 4 million have gone – 6 million to go.

b. Hitler declares that it is better for the whole German nation to die as a race of heroes on the battlefield than to abandon the ideals of the greater Reich.

c. Hitler has determined that the German people must share his personal fate – victory or destruction. Because honorable defeat is not possible for him, he will not permit it for Germany, but insists that the whole nation be utterly destroyed with him if he falls.

d. Hitler believes that air-raids are racially beneficial because they weed out the incompetents who cannot save themselves and the biological weaklings who break under the strain.

e. Hitler knew that the British and American air-raids were coming, but refused to make effective preparations because he believed that suffering from air-raids would stiffen the morale of the home front.

f. Hitler has ordered that air-raid victims who have been maimed and crippled be done away with by euthanasia. Also, old people who cannot stand the shock of air-raids and make a public nuisance of themselves.

g. Hitler will fight until the next-to-the-last German, and only then will sue for peace.

h. The total number of German casualties has never been revealed by Hitler. Civilians should demand the truth.

3. To spread the view that Hitler has gone insane.

Suggested Implementation:

a. Hitler's creeping paralysis ("progressive paralyse") due to syphilitic infection in the last war has now reached his speaking organs and his brain. When der Führer tried to rehearse a recent speech, it was discovered that he could not control his voice. Neither could he keep to the prepared text, but went off into wild and incoherent ramblings.

b. Hitler now raves that he will take a plane and follow Hess to England to argue the British out of the war. He is being closely guarded and will not be given access to a plane while his mind is still unbalanced.

c. Hitler hears voices every night and insists that Roehm is talking to him.

d. Hitler's insanity is now in the catatonic phase – he sits and stares all day long and has to be fed forcibly.

e. Dr. Jung, the Swiss psychiatrist, has washed his hands of Hitler's case.

f. The insulin shock treatment for insanity is being used on Hitler in order to restore his mind sufficiently so that he can make a speech.

g. Hitler now goes around all day dressed as Frederic the Great. He insisted on calling Goebbels Voltaire when the latter tried to approach him recently on a matter of state.

h. Hitler is now told only favorable news. His doctors fear a complete collapse should he be told the truth of Germany's situation.

i. Hitler now works out all his military strategy through star-gazing and occultism. He passes on his decisions to the generals who listen to him, promise they will do as he says and later report success. Actually, however, they pay no attention to the Führer whatsoever.

j. Hitler keeps two Jewish-Gypsy soothsayers with him at Berchtengaden all the time.

k. Hitler has spent the last month designing a stupendous mausoleum for himself.

l. Hitler has such delusions of persecution that he refuses to see anyone but his personal body guards, lives in a room without windows, and has his food tested before eating it.

m. At his last meeting with Himmler, Hitler screamed that even the SS had turned against him and were plotting against his life.

4. To spread the view that Hitler himself has completely lost faith in German victory.

Suggested Implementation:

a. Hitler staged a suicide attempt on September 3 by running a sword into his side. However, he missed hitting any vital organ and is well on the way to recovery.

b. Hitler refused to involve Spain in the war because he has a promise of sanctuary there when Germany is defeated.

c. Planes are kept ready at both Munich and Berlin air-ports for Hitler to flee the country. A special gasoline-carrying plane will allow the fugitives to make only one stop before reaching Japan.

d. Hitler grew furious when he read Roosevelt's note requesting neutral governments not to give asylum to Nazi leaders. Roosevelt apparently knew that Hitler and Goering were negotiating with both Spain and Turkey at the time.

e. Mussolini sent Hitler a post card from his island prison: "Having a lovely time. Bet you wish you were here." Hitler has confessed his envy of Mussolini.

5. To persuade left-wing National Socialists that Hitler has betrayed the socialist line.

Suggested Implementation:

a. For the last six months, Hitler has personally refused to speak or have anything to do with labor representatives. He insists that the "masses" approach him through the proper intermediaries.

b. Hitler's cronies who visit and feast with him at his retreats are now only industrialists and Junkers (names).

c. Hitler has taken up drinking French champagne and wears a monocle when at private parties with his industrialist and Junker friends. His clothes are all fashioned by a Parisian tailor.

d. Hitler is now pleased with the thought that he is socially acceptable.

e. Hitler agreed with the industrialists to use foreign laborers in Germany as a weapon to break the power of German labor and reduce their standard of living.

f. The growing monopolistic control of Germany economy is the result of a plan evolved by Hitler in 1935.

6. To spread the view that the Army and the industrialists have sold Germany down the river, and to create a demand that Hitler be given absolute and complete control of the German military and economic machine.

a. The Herrenklub is now running Germany ("die feine Herren sind wiedar da"). The Junkers, the industrialists and the SS have stabbed Germany in the back. Roehm was right. Hitler admits it now.

b. It is the timorous Junker generals, not Hitler, who made the colossal strategic errors, and are still doing so. If the generals had not refused to invade England in 1940 when Hitler wanted to, the war would now be over. Likewise, Russia would now be shattered if the generals had not got cold feet in the drive to Moscow. Let the Führer run the war, not the monocled, spiritless generals.

c. Hitler is being kept a virtual prisoner by the SS and the Junkers. His recent attempts to revitalize the SA were quickly blocked.

LUFTPOST

Von der Royal Air Force abgeworfen

Nr. 23
21. Oktober 1941

Verboten überall, wo die Wahrheit verboten ist

Russlands zweite Linie kampfbereit

LENINS Leichnam ist aus dem Moskauer Mausoleum am Roten Platz nach einer anderen Ruhestätte im Innern Russlands überführt worden.

Schon lange vorher sind andere Transporte nach dem Osten gegangen. Denn Russland kämpft weiter, gleichviel, wie die Schlacht um Moskau enden wird.

Ein grosser Teil des Maschinenparks der bedrohten Kriegsindustrien im europäischen Russland ist schon ins Innere Asiens geschafft worden. Mit ihm sind viele Facharbeiter und ihre Familien zu den neuen Produktionsstätten gewandert, u.a. nach Sverdlovsk, Tscheljabinsk und Magnetogorsk, wo neue Flugzeuge, neue Panzer gebaut, neue Geschütze gegossen werden.

Denn Stalin hat schon vor Jahren die Gefahr eines deutschen Angriffs erkannt. Und er hat gehandelt. Östlich des Urals sind neue Kriegsindustrien entstanden. Hier werden die Erze des Urals, die Kohle des Beckens von Kusnetz und die Baumwolle von Turkestan verarbeitet.

Und hinter dem schützenden Wall des Urals, unerreichbar für die Luftwaffe, werden die neuen Armeen der Sowjetunion aufgestellt, ausgerüstet und für den Kampf geschult. Denn der Kampf geht weiter, wie oft auch Hitler ihn für entschieden erklärt.

Was nicht weggeschafft werden konnte aus dem Gebiet, das dem Feind überlassen werden musste, haben die Russen zerstört. Allein in der Ukraine waren 90 000 landwirtschaftliche Traktoren in Betrieb. Sie sind nicht mehr vorhanden. Deutschland kann sie nicht ersetzen; denn es hat selbst nur 140 000 Traktoren. Und die Fabriken, die im Frieden Traktoren herstellten, bauen jetzt Panzer. Selbst wenn Deutschland sie ersetzen könnte: es hat nicht die Millionen von Hektolitern Benzin, die diese Maschinen jährlich verbrauchen.

Deutschland, das heute 3½ Millionen Ausländer und Gefangene beschäftigen muss, um seine Wirtschaft in Gang zu halten, hat auch nicht die Arbeitskräfte, die für die Ausbeutung des eroberten Gebietes benötigt werden. Noch weniger hat es die Rohstoffe und Menschen, um im Krieg all das wieder aufzubauen, was ein entschlossener Gegner vernichtet hat.

DER BISCHOF VON MÜNSTER KLAGT AN

SEITE 3

Ein französischer Seemann wird als Geisel in Vincennes erschossen. Nach der Ermordung des deutschen Kommandanten von Nantes, Oberst-Leutnant Holtz, wurden am 21. Oktober 50 Geiseln erschossen. Falls die wirklichen Täter nicht innerhalb von 2 Tagen verhaftet werden können, sollen weitere 50 unschuldige Geiseln erschossen werden. (Siehe „Unsere Meinung" S.2)

Ohne Ausbildung an den Feind

U-570, das sich am 25. August 1941 südlich von Island einem britischen Hudson-Flugzeug ergab, hatte eine Besatzung von 44 Mann.

Davon waren 42, also alle ausser dem Ingenieur-Leutnant und dem Stabssteuermann, zum ersten Male auf Feindfahrt. Nicht einmal der Kommandant hatte Kriegserfahrung.

Einen Monat vorher hatte die gleiche Besatzung auf der Fahrt von Trondheim nach dem Bug und das Hörgerät des U-Boots durch ein überstürztes Schnelltauchmanöver, bei dem das Boot auf ein Riff auflief, schwer beschädigt.

Fast die gesamte Besatzung war seekrank, infolge von mangelnder Erfahrung auf hoher See.

★   ★   ★

In einem U-Boot im aktiven Dienst bildet ein einziger unerfahrener Offizier oder Unteroffizier eine dauernde Gefahr für das Schiff und die Besatzung. Durch die Entsendung dieses U-Bootes, das fast durchweg mit Anfängern bemannt war, hatte die deutsche Flottenleitung die Mannschaft zum Tode verurteilt.

Versicherungsgesellschaften in neutralen Ländern bemessen die durchschnittliche Lebensaussicht eines deutschen U-Boot-matrosen im aktiven Dienst auf 62 Tage.

DIE MORDKOMMISSION GREIFT WEITER

Deutsche Bergleute, die bisher unabkömmlich waren, müssen jetzt einrücken.

Deutschland braucht all die Kohle die es fördern kann, für den Bedarf seiner Industrie, für die Gewinnung künstlichen Benzins, für die Versorgung Italiens und für Hausbrand. Aber noch dringender wird es für neue Soldaten gebraucht, die die Toten an der Ostfront ersetzen sollen.

510 x

Luftpost ('Airmail'), a four-page miniature newspaper dropped by the RAF. Issue number 23, of 21 October 1941, contained stories on the stiffening of Soviet resistance; problems with oil; the execution of a French seaman; a speech by Bishop Galen of Münster contradicting the official Nazi party line; and a graph showing Allied bombing targets. Interestingly there is an early mention of the US 'Flying Fortress' B-17, which was actually flown by the RAF over Europe in the summer of 1941 before the United States entered the war. One piece is credited to Sefton Delmer, former Beaverbrook newspaper 'Chief European correspondent', and by this time covert lynchpin of the 'Political Warfare Executive' ('PWE') in London.

[OVERLEAF] FÜR FÜHRER UND VATERLAND – WARUM?

'For Fuhrer and Fatherland – Why?', c.1942–3, an unattributed leaflet pointing out the futility of German military sacrifice, showed dead soldiers in the snow against a background of death notices. The text to the rear declares that 'Hitler can no longer win the war', the combined industrial production of Britain, Russia and America being vastly superior. 'New Millions' will have to die for Hitler. Though fairly obviously a Western Allied production, the specific attack on Nazi policy and apparent empathy with the loss of the 'German people' is an interesting, and very deliberate, twist on less sophisticated messages.

Für Führer und Vaterland

Warum?

Ende des Krieges verhältnismäßig gemütlich bei leichtem in der Garnison abwarten. Ein schwerer Fall dieser Krankheit es völlig unmöglich, daß der Betroffene schwere Arbeit Mit ein bischen Glück kannst du schließlich erreichen, daß du em Wehrdienst entlassen wirst.

lweise Lähmung.

ier angegebenen Maßnahmen haben eine gewisse Ähnlichkeit en unter 1 angeführten. Du mußt aber verstehen, daß zwischen ein grundsätzlicher Unterschied besteht. Die Nuß, von der wir zelprochen haben, war nur ein mechanisches Hilfsmittel, um dir tige Art, dich zu bewegen, beizubringen. Auch im Folgenden s sich um kleine, runde Gegenstände handeln, die an verschiedenen t des Körpers durch Binden in der richtigen Lage gehalten n müssen. Der Zweck hierbei aber ist, eine tatsächliche Krankscheinung hervorzurufen, nicht nur ihre Nachahmung zu en.

ung eines Armes oder Beins ist natürlich eine Beschwerde, auf kein Arzt vermeiden kann, den betreffenden Mann krank zu en, und zwar mindestens so lange, wie die Lähmung andauert. Lähmung zu simulieren, ist so gut wie unmöglich. Jeder Doktor einen Mann, der behauptet, gelähmt zu sein, ohne daß er es) ist, schnell hereinlegen.

nicht schwer, eine wirkliche Lähmung hervorzurufen, von der st nicht feststellen kann, woher sie kommt, und die er als eine fte Krankheit anerkennen muß. Diese Beschwerde hat den Vorteil, daß sie keinerlei schauspielerisches Talent erfordert. treffende Mann hat weiter nichts zu tun, als die hier gegebenen äge zu befolgen, und dann zum Arzt zu gehen und ihm die eit zu sagen. (Er darf natürlich bloß nie herauskommen lassen, getan hat, um die Beschwerde hervorzurufen. Aber so idiotisch a wohl niemand sein.)

angen dieser Art können an verschiedenen Stellen hervorgerufen . Das Prinzip ist immer dasselbe: Wenn man für einige inen dauernden Druck auf einen Nerv ausübt, dann beginnt ner Weile der Nerv auf kürzere oder längere Zeit zu streiken.

Die Nerven sind gewissermaßen die Telephonleitungen, über die das Gehirn seine Befehle an die Muskeln durchgibt. Wenn die Leitung unterbrochen ist, können die betreffenden Muskeln, die „angeschlossen" sind, eben keine Bewegungen machen. In Wirklichkeit können solche „Unterbrechungen der Leitung" aus allen möglichen Gründen hervorgerufen werden. Das braucht dich nicht zu kümmern. Laß ruhig den Doktor sich darüber den Kopf zerbrechen, was in deinem Fall der Grund sein könnte. Du weißt es selber natürlich auch nicht, und kannst ihm „leider" nicht helfen. An der Tatsache, daß das betreffende Glied gelähmt ist, kann keiner zweifeln, aus dem einfachen Grunde, weil es wirklich gelähmt sein wird.

Wo die Nerven liegen, auf die der Druck ausgeübt werden muß, siehst du aus den Abbildungen 8, 9 und 10. An diesen Stellen wirst

Abbildung 8.

A) Der Nerv am „Musikantenknochen", angezeigt durch den Kreis am Ende der gestrichelten Linie. (Rechter Arm.)

B) Derselbe Nerv, am linken Arm mit angedeuteter Haudlage.

du mit einigem Suchen den Nerv fühlen können. Er fühlt sich an wie ein dünner Strick und ist natürlich auf Druck empfindlich.

Das bekannteste Beispiel ist der Nerv, der über den sogenannten „Musikantenknochen" läuft. (Abbildung 8.) Der Nerv liegt hier dicht unter der Haut an der inneren Seite der Ellbogenspitze. Bekanntlich ruft schon ein leichter Stoß an dieser Stelle das bekannte Schmerzgefühl

35

[ABOVE] MALINGERERS CHARTER, c.1942

A feature in the booklet Krankheit Rettet ('Illness Saves') showing how temporary paralysis could be produced in an arm. This was just one of a number of Allied clandestine publications encouraging malingering among enemy service personnel and foreign workers. Other examples were translated into a variety of languages and camouflaged under the covers of hymn books, railway timetables, guidebooks, dictionaries and official instructions. Some of the techniques were printed onto cigarette papers, small and light enough easily to be left inside books or in other strategic places, or passed around with minimum danger. The idea was the brainchild of Dr John McCurdy, Cambridge lecturer in psycopathology, and many of the methods were tested experimentally in the UK before distribution. Foreign workers were also given suggestions on faking prescriptions and other documents, and how to behave in an interview with a doctor.

DE Wervelwind

Maandblad voor vrijheid, waarheid en recht

1ste JAARGANG • No. 2 • MEI 1942

WAT OOK VAL, TROUW STAAT PAL

[OPPOSITE] DE WERVELWIND, 1942

The Wervelwind *Dutch patriotic magazine proudly proclaimed that it was
'delivered by the RAF', but a format slightly smaller than a postcard made
it highly suitable for concealment and passing on. The contents of this
second edition, May 1942, included a piece on a speech by the Dutch
Queen; resistance in the Dutch Indies and Balkans; and German financial
plundering. A lengthy section was devoted to the RAF air offensives, and
the Halifax bomber. Crucial was an article on how to make your own
radio, and the frequencies used by the BBC and other free world stations.
In May 1943 the Nazi propaganda leader, Joseph Goebbels, would
confide to his diary that he believed that 'British propaganda' was behind
industrial unrest: he therefore advocated 'taking radio sets away from the
Dutch as quickly as possible'.*

[OVERLEAF] AN INVITATION TO DESERTION, 1943

*A fake poster of 1943, sporting an apparently official stamp and the
name of General von Falkenhorst, German commander in Norway, which
suggests that deserters in Sweden are allowed to remain there if they are
in civilian clothing and have been there for more than 24 hours. In reality
it was a British 'black' operation to encourage desertion and undermine
morale. Other bogus documents encouraged enemy combatants to escape
to Spain and Switzerland, or painted rosy pictures of the conditions of
prisoners of war in the United States and Canada. Items such as these
were relatively easy to create: forging identity papers was often much
more tricky – less because any one document was difficult to replicate,
but because the systems being copied were complicated and could be
changed.*

DEUTSCHER SOLDAT!

DIE schimpfliche Zunahme der Fälle, in denen Mannschaften und sogar Offiziere der mir unterstellten Einheiten und Dienststellen sich ihrer Wehrverpflichtung durch Übertritt auf schwedisches Gebiet entzogen haben, gibt mir Veranlassung, auf Folgendes hinzuweisen:

1.) Wenn auch die Strafbestimmungen für das ehrlose Verbrechen der Fahnenflucht (§ 6 KSStV) Tod oder Zuchthaus vorsehen, so ist doch in der Praxis die Strafe immer Tod.

2.) Fahnenflucht ist nicht nur ein ehrloses Verbrechen, sondern auch ein fast aussichtsloses Unterfangen. Entgegen gewissen, vom Feind verbreiteten Gerüchten, besteht in Schweden kein Asylrecht für deutsche Wehrmachtangehörige, die innerhalb 24 Stunden nach Überschreiten der Grenze oder in Uniform von der schwedischen Polizei auf schwedischem Boden aufgegriffen werden. Solche Fahnenflüchtige werden unverzüglich an die nächste deutsche Dienststelle ausgeliefert.

Nach den geltenden Bestimmungen wird Asylrecht nur solchen Personen gewährt, die Zivilkleider tragen oder deren Kleidung nicht als die international anerkannte Uniform eines deutschen Wehrmachtteils identifiziert werden kann, und die sich länger als 24 Stunden in Schweden aufgehalten haben.

3.) Allen Wehrmachtangehörigen wird zur Pflicht gemacht, mit allen Kräften daran mitzuarbeiten, daß das wachsende Übel der Fahnenflucht ausgerottet wird. In diesem kritischen Augenblick höchster Bereitschaft und höchster Gefahr kommt es auf jeden Einzelnen an.

Der Militärbefehlshaber
für die besetzten norwegischen Gebiete
(gez.) von Falkenhorst
Generaloberst.

Oslo, 18. 2. 1943.

Münchner Neueste Nachrichten

Wirtschaftsblatt, Alpine und Sport-Zeitung

1941 wird das Jahr des Endsieges werden

Der Neujahrsbefehl des Führers an die Wehrmacht

Das Jahr des Herkules

EIN PEINLICHES VERSPRECHEN !

[ABOVE] HITLER'S PREDICTION OF VICTORY, 1941–2

Ein Peinliches Versprechen! ('An Embarrassing Promise!'). A British air-dropped propaganda leaflet pointing out that Hitler had prophesied 1941 as the year of 'final victory'. This was just one of many different messages intended to spread increasing unease amongst the German civilian population as the war dragged on. Undermining the Führer myth through 'black' propaganda and clandestine means would become one of the stated objectives of OSS.

NACHR

Schlacht um e

Die Sowjets erobern Reval

Die grosse Hafenstadt Reval, die Hauptstadt Estlands, wurde gestern von den Sowjets genommen.

Sowjetpanzer stiessen von Wesenberg in einem Tage 100 km vor und drangen in Reval ein, wo man gerade mit Räumungsmassnahmen begonnen hatte. Nur wenige Spezialisten und Verwaltungsoffiziere konnten noch rechtzeitig auf dem

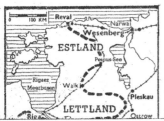

8 000 Mann er sich in Boul

Die schwersten Kämpfe se schlachten in der Normand zwischen Nimwegen und Arnh um das Einfallstor nach dem der Norddeutschen Tiefebene.

Die deutschen Truppen haben Preis die englischen Panzer, die b Südarm des Rheins überquert hab zurückzuwerfen.

Alles wird eingesetzt, um zu verhinder nach Arnheim durchstossen und die Verb landetruppen herstellen, die hier schon s starken Brückenkopf am Nordufer des gegen alle Angriffe halten.

Ein klares Kampfbild lässt sich nicht gewinnen, denn überall zwischen Nimwegen und Arnheim sind deutsche und alliierte Truppen durcheinander gewürfelt.

Nach letzten Meldungen hat die Pak die britische Panzerspitze, die nach Arnheim durch will, nördlich Nimwegen zum Stehen gebracht.

und Emm gebiet;

2. im R Köln und

3. zwisc Trier gege

4. zwisc gegen die

Aus de und Trier

Rheinbrücken

**Kessel-
n jetzt
Holland
iet und**

im jeden
egen den
imwegen

Engländer
den Luft-
gen einen
Rheinarms

das Ruhr-

chen gegen

Eifel und
; und
nd Belfort
Oberrhein.
n Aachen
merikaner

Weniger V1 im Einsatz gegen England

Die Tatsache, dass der Beschuss Südenglands und des Raumes von Gross-London durch die V 1-Waffe nicht mehr fortlaufend in dem amtlichen deutschen Wehrmachtbericht Erwähnung findet, wird, laut DNB., in militärischen Kreisen der Reichshauptstadt damit erklärt, dass

[PREVIOUS PAGES] NEWS FOR THE TROOPS, 1944

Nachricten Für Die Truppe ('News for the Troops'), No. 160. Printed on newspaper presses at Luton in the UK, this daily journal had the superficial appearance of a German production for its own fighting personnel. In reality it was an Anglo-American 'black' propaganda exercise. Its contents were genuine news stories, culled partly from official enemy sources, mixed together with 'subversive' opinion and scurrilous tit-bits about Nazi leaders, both true and false. As one genuine German newspaper observed, articles that tallied fairly closely with other sources 'lulled the reader's suspicions'. Produced very rapidly, in issues of 250,000 to 750,000 copies, it was dropped over enemy-held areas of Western Europe by US aircraft during the latter part of the war. At the time of D-Day this was one of four key 'covert' propaganda operations. Two others were broadcast based, being the Soldatensender Calais, and the SS 'opposition' radio, both of which also posed as German. The fourth operation was the production and distribution of various documents and leaflets, by agents and balloons, to promote defeatist attitudes and rumour.

The Nachrichten edition of 23 September 1944 spoke of the Soviet capture of Tallinn in Estonia, the threat posed by the assault at Nimegen, and the surrender of 8,000 German troops at Boulogne. Though many quickly realized that the paper was an Allied production it was still quite widely read because in most battlefield areas news of any description was difficult to obtain. It was deemed sufficiently troublesome to merit space in German newspapers and military reports refuting its allegations.

SIMPLE SABOTAGE
FIELD MANUAL, 1944

STRATEGIC SERVICES FIELD MANUAL NO. 3

OSS

The popular picture of the 'secret army' in World War II is of derailed trains, blown bridges, ambushed staff cars, escaping prisoners and mountain hideouts. Yet the work of OSS and SOE also involved convincing local populations that the Allies were going to win, giving them hope of eventual liberation, and encouraging them not to co-operate with the enemy. Simple sabotage gave patriotic Europeans methods of subtle non-compliance, shoddy workmanship, relatively low-risk meddling and passive resistance that many could indulge. The German use of foreign labour that wasted time and failed to make effective munitions could prove counter productive. The text reproduced here, as it stands, was used in the training of agents – its messages were carried to practitioners in translations, leaflets, broadcasts, locally produced papers, and by word of mouth within occupied Europe.

The logic of simple sabotage is difficult to dispute, for the enemy was hugely dependent on foreign labour. Czechs had been employed before 1939, and in 1944 the *International Labour Review* suggested that there were more than 6,000,000 foreign workers in Germany alone, with millions more on war-related production in their own countries. Even without sabotage, this huge labour force needed organisation, supervision and direction, and by 1942 'voluntary' recruitment was drying up. The minor sabotage of recruitment agencies proved particularly effective when they were bombarded with pointless enquiries, inaccurate information, and suffered loss of vital paperwork. Longer hours, Sunday work, new laws against malingering and armed and uniformed factory guards became the order of the day. German Armaments Minister Albert Speer later recalled that the 'solution of the labour problem' was his most pressing issue. But with Hitler demanding the full exploitation of conquered populations there was little that could be done, 'to prevent enemy sabotage services from planting agents'.

Office of Strategic Services
Washington D.C.
17 January 1944

This Simple Sabotage Field Manual – Strategic Services (Provisional) – is published for the information and guidance of all concerned and will be used as the basic doctrine for Strategic Services training for this subject.

The contents of this Manual should be carefully controlled and should not be allowed to come into unauthorized hands.

The instructions may be placed in separate pamphlets or leaflets according to categories of operations but should be distributed with care and not broadly. They should be used as a basis of radio broadcasts only for local and special cases and as directed by the theater commander.

AR 380-5, pertaining to handling of secret documents, will be complied with in the handling of this Manual.

William J. Donovan

1. INTRODUCTION

a. The purpose of this paper is to characterize simple sabotage, to outline its possible effects, and to present suggestions for inciting and executing it.

b. Sabotage varies from highly technical coup de main acts that require detailed planning and the use of specially trained operatives, to innumerable simple acts which the ordinary individual citizen-saboteur can perform. This paper is primarily concerned with the latter type. Simple sabotage does not require specially prepared tools or equipment; it is executed by an ordinary citizen who may or may not act individually and without the necessity for active connection with an organized group; and it is carried out in such a way as to involve a minimum danger of injury, detection, and reprisal.

c. Where destruction is involved, the weapons of the citizen-saboteur are salt, nails, candles, pebbles, thread, or any other materials he might normally be expected to possess as a householder or as a worker in his particular occupation. His arsenal is the kitchen shelf, the trash pile, his own usual kit of tools and supplies. The targets of his sabotage are usually objects to which he has normal and inconspicuous access in everyday life.

d. A second type of simple sabotage requires no destructive tools whatsoever and produces physical damage, if any, by highly indirect means. It is based on universal opportunities to make faulty decisions, to adopt a non-cooperative attitude, and to induce others to follow suit. Making a faulty decision may be simply a matter of placing tools in one spot instead of another. A non-cooperative attitude may involve nothing more than creating an unpleasant situation among one's fellow workers, engaging in bickerings, or displaying surliness and stupidity.

e. This type of activity, sometimes referred to as the "human element," is frequently responsible for accidents, delays, and general obstruction even under normal conditions. The potential saboteur should discover what types of faulty decisions and operation are normally found in this kind of work and should then devise his sabotage so as to enlarge that "margin for error."

2. POSSIBLE EFFECTS

a. Acts of simple sabotage are occurring throughout Europe. An effort should be made to add to their efficiency, lessen their detectability, and increase their number. Acts of simple sabotage, multiplied by thousands of citizen-saboteurs, can be an effective weapon against the enemy. Slashing tires, draining fuel tanks, starting fires, starting arguments, acting stupidly, short-circuiting electric systems, abrading machine parts will waste materials, manpower, and time. Occurring on a wide scale, simple sabotage will be a constant and tangible drag on the war effort of the enemy.

b. Simple sabotage may also have secondary results of more or less value. Widespread practice of simple sabotage will harass and demoralize enemy administrators and police. Further, success may embolden the citizen-saboteur eventually to find colleagues who can assist him in sabotage of greater dimensions. Finally, the very practice of simple sabotage by natives in enemy or occupied territory may make these individuals identify themselves actively with the United Nations war effort, and encourage them to assist openly in periods of Allied invasion and occupation.

3. MOTIVATING THE SABOTEUR

a. To incite the citizen to the active practice of simple sabotage and to keep him practicing that sabotage over sustained periods is a special problem.

b. Simple sabotage is often an act which the citizen performs according to his own initiative and inclination. Acts of destruction do not bring him any personal gain and may be completely foreign to his habitually conservationist attitude toward materials and tools. Purposeful stupidity is contrary to human nature. He frequently needs pressure, stimulation or assurance, and information and suggestions regarding feasible methods of simple sabotage.

(1) Personal Motives

(a) The ordinary citizen very probably has no immediate personal motive for committing simple sabotage. Instead, he must be made to anticipate indirect personal gain, such as might come with enemy evacuation or destruction of the ruling government group. Gains should be stated as specifically as possible for the area addressed: simple sabotage will hasten the day when Commissioner X and his deputies Y and Z will be thrown out, when particularly obnoxious decrees and restrictions will be abolished, when food will arrive, and so on. Abstract verbalizations about personal liberty, freedom of the press, and so on, will not be convincing in most parts of the world. In many areas they will not even be comprehensible.

(b) Since the effect of his own acts is limited, the saboteur may become discouraged unless he feels that he is a member of a large, though unseen, group of saboteurs operating against the enemy or the government of his own country and elsewhere. This can be conveyed indirectly: suggestions which he reads and hears can include observations that a particular technique has been successful in this or that district. Even if the technique is not applicable to his surroundings, another's success will encourage him to attempt similar acts. It also can be conveyed directly: statements praising the effectiveness of simple sabotage can be contrived which will be published by white radio, freedom stations, and the subversive press. Estimates of the proportion of the population engaged in sabotage can be disseminated. Instances of successful sabotage already are being broadcast by white radio and freedom stations, and this should be continued and expanded where compatible with security.

(c) More important than (a) or (b) would be to create a situation in which the citizen-saboteur acquires a sense of responsibility and begins to educate others in simple sabotage.

(2) Encouraging Destructiveness

It should be pointed out to the saboteur where the circumstances are suitable, that he is acting in self-defense against the enemy, or retaliating against the enemy for other acts of destruction. A reasonable amount of humor in the presentation of suggestions for simple sabotage will relax tensions of fear.

(a) The saboteur may have to reverse his thinking, and he should be told this in so many words. Where he formerly thought of keeping his tools sharp, he should now let them grow dull; surfaces that formerly were lubricated now should be sanded; normally diligent, he should now be lazy and careless; and so on. Once he is encouraged to think backwards about himself and the objects of his everyday life, the saboteur will see many opportunities in his immediate environment which cannot possibly be seen from a distance. A state of mind should be encouraged that anything can be sabotaged.

(b) Among the potential citizen-saboteurs who are to engage in physical destruction, two extreme types may be distinguished. On the one hand, there is the man who is not technically trained and employed. This man needs specific suggestions as to what he can and should destroy as well as details regarding the tools by means of which destruction is accomplished.

(c) At the other extreme is the man who is a technician, such as a lathe operator or an automobile mechanic. Presumably this man would be able to devise methods of simple sabotage which would be appropriate to his own facilities. However, this man needs to be stimulated to re-orient his thinking in the direction of destruction. Specific examples, which need not be from his own field, should accomplish this.

(d) Various media may be used to disseminate suggestions and information regarding simple sabotage. Among the media which may be used, as the immediate situation dictates, are: freedom stations or radio, false or offical leaflets. Broadcasts or leaflets may be directed toward specific geographic or occupational areas, or they may be general in scope. Finally, agents may be trained in the art of simple sabotage, in anticipation of a time when they may be able to communicate this information directly.

(3) Safety Measures

(a) The amount of activity carried on by the saboteur will be governed not only by the number of opportunities he sees, but also by the amount of danger he feels. Bad news travels fast, and simple sabotage will be discouraged if too many simple saboteurs are arrested.

(b) It should not be difficult to prepare leaflets and other media for the saboteur about the choice of weapons, time, and targets which will insure the saboteur against detection and retaliation. Among such suggestions might be the following:

(1) Use materials which appear to be innocent. A knife or a nail file can be carried normally on your person; either is a multi-purpose instrument for creating damage. Matches, pebbles, hair, salt, nails, and dozens of other destructive agents can be carried or kept in your living quarters without exciting any suspicion whatever. If you are a worker in a particular trade or industry you can easily carry and keep such things as wrenches, hammers, emery paper, and the like.

(2) Try to commit acts for which large numbers of people could be responsible. For instance, if you blow out the wiring in a factory at a central fuze box, almost anyone could have done it. On-the-street sabotage after dark, such as you might be able to carry out against a military car or truck, is another example of an act for which it would be impossible to blame you.

(3) Do not be afraid to commit acts for which you might be blamed directly, so long as you do so rarely, and as long as you have a plausible excuse: you dropped your wrench across an electric circuit because an air raid had kept you up the night before and you were half-dozing at work. Always be profuse in your apologies. Frequently you can "get away" with such acts under the cover of pretending stupidity, ignorance, over-caution, fear of being suspected of sabotage, or weakness and dullness due to undernourishment.

(4) After you have committed an act of easy sabotage, resist any temptation to wait around and see what happens. Loiterers arouse suspicion. Of course, there are circumstances when it would be suspicious for you to leave. If you commit sabotage on your job, you should naturally stay at your work.

4. TOOLS, TARGETS, AND TIMING

(a) The citizen-saboteur cannot be closely controlled. Nor is it reasonable to expect that simple sabotage can be precisely concentrated on specific types of target according to the requirements of a concrete military situation. Attempts to control simple sabotage according to developing military factors, moreover, might provide the enemy with intelligence of more or less value in anticipating the date and area of notably intensified or notably slackened military activity.

(b) Sabotage suggestions, of course, should be adapted to fit the area where they are to be practiced. Target priorities for general types of situations likewise can be specified, for emphasis at the proper time by the underground press, freedom stations, and cooperating propaganda.

(1) Under General Conditions

(**a**) Simple sabotage is more than malicious mischief, and it should always consist of acts whose results will be detrimental to the materials and manpower of the enemy.

(**b**) The saboteur should be ingenious in using his every-day equipment. All sorts of weapons will present themselves if he looks at his surroundings in a different light. For example, emery dust – a powerful weapon – may at first seem unobtainable, but if the saboteur were to pulverize an enemy knife sharpener or emery wheel with a hammer, he would find himself with a plentiful supply.

(**c**) The saboteur should never attack targets beyond his capacity or the capacity of his instruments. An inexperienced person should not, for example, attempt to use explosives, but should confine himself to the use of matches or other familiar weapons.

(**d**) The saboteur should try to damage only objects and materials known to be in use by the enemy or to be destined for early use by the enemy. It will be safe for him to assume that almost any product of heavy industry is destined for enemy use, and that the most efficient fuels and lubricants also are destined for enemy use. Without special knowledge, however, it would be undesirable for him to attempt destruction of food crops or food products.

(**e**) Although the citizen-saboteur may rarely have access to military objects, he should give these preference above all others.

(2) Prior to a Military Offensive

During periods which are quiescent in a military sense, such emphasis as can be given to simple sabotage might well center on industrial production, to lessen the flow of materials and equipment to the enemy. Slashing a rubber tire on an Army truck may be an act of value; spoiling a batch of rubber in the production plant is an act of still more value.

(3) During a Military Offensive

(a) Most significant sabotage for an area which is, or is soon destined to be, a theater of combat operations is that whose effects will be direct and immediate. Even if the effects are relatively minor and localized, this type of sabotage is to be preferred to activities whose effects, while widespread, are indirect and delayed.

(1) The saboteur should be encouraged to attack transportation faculties of all kinds. Among such facilities are roads, railroads, automobiles, trucks, motor-cycles, bicycles, trains, and trams.

(2) Any communications facilities which can be used by the authorities to transmit instructions or morale material should be the objects of simple sabotage. These include telephone, telegraph and power systems, radio, newspapers, placards, and public notices.

(3) Critical materials, valuable in themselves or necessary to the efficient functioning of transportation and communication, also should become targets for the citizen-saboteur. These may include oil, gasoline, tires, food, and water.

5. SPECIFIC SUGGESTIONS FOR SIMPLE SABOTAGE

(a) It will not be possible to evaluate the desirability of simple sabotage in an area without having in mind rather specifically what individual acts and results are embraced by the definition of simple sabotage.

(b) A listing of specific acts follows, classified according to types of target. This list is presented as a growing rather than a complete outline of the methods of simple sabotage. As new techniques are developed, or new fields explored, it will be elaborated and expanded.

(1) Buildings

Warehouses, barracks, offices, hotels, and factory buildings are outstanding targets for simple sabotage. They are extremely susceptible to damage, especially by fire; they offer opportunities to such untrained people as janitors, charwomen, and casual visitors; and, when damaged, they present a relatively large handicap to the enemy.

(a) Fires can be started wherever there is an accumulation of inflammable material. Warehouses are obviously the most promising targets but incendiary sabotage need not be confined to them alone.

(1) Whenever possible, arrange to have the fire start after you have gone away. Use a candle and paper combination, setting it as close as possible to the inflamable material you want to burn: From a sheet of paper, tear a strip three or four centimeters wide and wrap it around the base of the candle two or three times. Twist more sheets of paper into loose ropes and place them around the base of the candle. When the candle flame reaches the encircling strip, it will be ignited and in turn will ignite the surrounding paper. The size, heat, and duration of the resulting flame will depend on how much paper you use and how much of it you can cramp in a small space.

(2) With a flame of this kind, do not attempt to ignite any but rather inflammable materials, such as cotton sacking. To light more resistant materials, use a candle plus tightly rolled or twisted paper which has been soaked in gasoline. To create a

briefer but even hotter flame, put celluloid such as you might find in an old comb, into a nest of plain or saturated paper which is to be fired by a candle.

(3) To make another type of simple fuse, soak one end of a piece of string in grease. Rub a generous pinch of gunpowder over the inch of string where greasy string meets clean string. Then ignite the clean end of the string. It will burn slowly without a flame (in much the same way that a cigarette burns) until it reaches the grease and gunpowder; it will then flare up suddenly. The grease-treated string will then burn with a flame. The same effect may be achieved by using matches instead of the grease and gunpowder. Run the string over the match heads, taking care that the string is not pressed or knotted. They too will produce a sudden flame. The advantage of this type of fuse is that string burns at a set speed. You can time your fire by the length and thickness of the string you chose.

(4) Use a fuse such as the ones suggested above to start a fire in an office after hours. The destruction of records and other types of documents would be a serious handicap to the enemy.

(5) In basements where waste is kept, janitors should accumulate oily and greasy waste. Such waste sometimes ignites spontaneously, but it can easily be lit with a cigarette or match. If you are a janitor on night duty, you can be the first to report the fire, but don't report it too soon.

(6) A clean factory is not susceptible to fire, but a dirty one is. Workers should be careless with refuse and janitors should be inefficient in cleaning. If enough dirt and trash can be accumulated an otherwise fireproof building will become inflammable.

(7) Where illuminating gas is used in a room which is vacant at night, shut the windows tightly, turn on the gas, and leave a candle burning in the room, closing the door tightly behind you. After a time, the gas will explode, and a fire may or may not follow.

(b) Water and miscellaneous

(1) Ruin warehouse stock by setting the automatic sprinkler system to work. You can do this by tapping the sprinkler heads sharply with a hammer or by holding a match under them.

(2) Forget to provide paper in toilets; put tightly rolled paper, hair, and other obstructions in the W. C. Saturate a sponge with a thick starch or sugar solution. Squeeze it tightly into a ball, wrap it with string, and dry. Remove the string when fully dried. The sponge will be in the form of a tight hard ball. Flush down a W. C. or otherwise introduce into a sewer line. The sponge will gradually expand to its normal size and plug the sewage system.

(3) Put a coin beneath a bulb in a public building during the daytime, so that fuses will blow out when lights are turned on at night. The fuses themselves may be rendered ineffective by putting a coin behind them or loading them with heavy wire. Then a short-circuit may either start a fire, damage transformers, or blow out a central fuse which will interrupt distribution of electricity to a large area.

(4) Jam paper, bits of wood, hairpins, and anything else that will fit, into the locks of all unguarded entrances to public buildings.

(2) Industrial Production: Manufacturing

(a) **Tools**

(1) Let cutting tools grow dull. They will be inefficient, will slow down production, and may damage the materials and parts you use them on.

(2) Leave saws slightly twisted when you are not using them. After a while, they will break when used.

(3) Using a very rapid stroke will wear out a file before its time. So will dragging a file in slow strokes under heavy pressure. Exert pressure on the backward stroke as well as the forward stroke.

(4) Clean files by knocking them against the vise or the workpiece; they are easily broken this way.

(5) Bits and drills will snap under heavy pressure.

(6) You can put a press punch out of order by putting in it more material than it is adjusted for – two blanks instead of one, for example.

(7) Power-driven tools like pneumatic drills, riveters, and so on, are never efficient when dirty. Lubrication points and electric contacts can easily be fouled by normal accumulations of dirt or the insertion of foreign matter.

(b) Oil and lubrication systems are not only vulnerable to easy sabotage, but are critical in every machine with moving parts. Sabotage of oil and lubrication will slow production or stop work entirely at strategic points in industrial processes.

(1) Put metal dust or filings, fine sand, ground glass, emery

dust (get it by pounding up an emery knife sharpener) and similar hard, gritty substances directly into lubrication systems. They will scour smooth surfaces, ruining pistons, cylinder walls, shafts, and bearings. They will overheat and stop motors which will need overhauling, new parts, and extensive repairs. Such materials, if they are used, should be introduced into lubrication systems past any filters which otherwise would strain them out.

(2) You can cause wear on any machine by uncovering a filter system, poking a pencil or any other sharp object through the filter mesh, then covering it up again. Or, if you can dispose of it quickly, simply remove the filter.

(3) If you cannot get at the lubrication system or filter directly, you may be able to lessen the effectiveness of oil by diluting it in storage. In this case, almost any liquid will do which will thin the oil. A small amount of sulphuric acid, varnish, water-glass, or linseed oil will be especially effective.

(4) Using a thin oil where a heavy oil is prescribed will break down a machine or heat up a moving shaft so that it will "freeze" and stop.

(5) Put any clogging substance into lubrication systems or, if it will float, into stored oil. Twisted combings of human hair, pieces of string, dead insects, and many other common objects will be effective in stopping or hindering the flow of oil through feed lines and filters.

(6) Under some circumstances, you may be able to destroy oil outright rather than interfere with its effectiveness, by removing stop-plugs from lubricating systems or by puncturing the drums and cans in which it is stored.

(c) Cooling Systems

(1) A water cooling system can be put out of commission in a fairly short time, with considerable damage to an engine or motor, if you put into it several pinches of hard grain, such as rice or wheat. They will swell up and choke the circulation of water, and the cooling system will have to be torn down to remove the obstruction. Sawdust or hair may also be used to clog a water cooling system.

(2) If very cold water is quickly introduced into the cooling system of an overheated motor, contraction and considerable strain on the engine housing will result. If you can repeat the treatment a few times, cracking and serious damage will result.

(3) You can ruin the effectiveness of an air cooling system by plugging dirt and waste into intake or exhaust valves. If a belt-run fan is used in the system, make a jagged cut at least half way through the belt; it will slip and finally part under strain and the motor will overheat.

(d) Gasoline and Oil Fuel

Tanks and fueling engines usually are accessible and easy to open. They afford a very vulnerable target for simple sabotage activities.

(1) Put several pinches of sawdust or hard grain, such as rice or wheat, into the fuel tank of a gasoline engine. The particles will choke a feed line so that the engine will stop. Some time will be required to discover the source of the trouble. Although they will be hard to get, crumbs of natural rubber, such as you might find in old rubber bands and pencil erasers, are also effective.

(2) If you can accumulate sugar, put it in the fuel tank of a gasoline engine. As it burns together with the gasoline, it will turn into a sticky mess which will completely mire the engine and necessitate extensive cleaning and repair. Honey and molasses are as good as sugar. Try to use about 75–100 grams for each 10 gallons of gasoline.

(3) Other impurities which you can introduce into gasoline will cause rapid engine wear and eventual breakdown. Fine particles of pumice, sand, ground glass, and metal dust can easily be introduced into a gasoline tank. Be sure that the particles are very fine, so that they will be able to pass through the carburetor jet.

(4) Water, urine, wine, or any other simple liquid you can get in reasonably large quantities will dilute gasoline fuel to a point where no combustion will occur in the cylinder and the engine will not move. One pint to 20 gallons of gasoline is sufficient. If salt water is used, it will cause corrosion and permanent motor damage.

(5) In the case of Diesel engines, put low flashpoint oil into the fuel tank; the engine will not move. If there already is proper oil in the tank when the wrong kind is added, the engine will only limp and sputter along.

(6) Fuel lines to gasoline and oil engines frequently pass over the exhaust pipe. When the machine is at rest, you can stab a small hole in the fuel line and plug the hole with wax. As the engine runs and the exhaust tube becomes hot, the wax will be melted; fuel will drip onto the exhaust and a blaze will start.

(7) If you have access to a room where gasoline is stored, remember that gas vapor accumulating in a closed room will

explode after a time if you leave a candle burning in the room. A good deal of evaporation, however, must occur from the gasoline tins into the air of the room. If removal of the tops of the tins does not expose enough gasoline to the air to ensure copious evaporation, you can open lightly constructed tins further with a knife, ice pick or sharpened nail file. Or puncture a tiny hole in the tank which will permit gasoline to leak out on the floor. This will greatly increase the rate of evaporation. Before you light your candle, be sure that windows are closed and the room is as air-tight as you can make it. If you can see that windows in a neighboring room are opened wide, you have a chance of setting a large fire which will not only destroy the gasoline but anything else nearby; when the gasoline explodes, the doors of the storage room will be blown open, a draft to the neighboring windows will be created which will whip up a fine conflagration.

(e) Electric Motors

Electric motors (including dynamos) are more restricted than the targets so far discussed. They cannot be sabotaged easily or without risk of injury by unskilled persons who may otherwise have good opportunities for destruction.

(1) Set the rheostat to a high point of resistance in all types of electric motors. They will overheat and catch fire.

(2) Adjust the overload relay to a very high value beyond the capacity of the motor. Then overload the motor to a point where it will overheat and break down.

(3) Remember that dust, dirt, and moisture are enemies of electrical equipment. Spill dust and dirt onto the points where the wires in electric motors connect with terminals, and onto insulating parts. Inefficient transmission of

current and, in some cases, short circuits will result. Wet generator motors to produce short circuits.

(4) "Accidentally" bruise the insulation on wire, loosen nuts on connections, make faulty splices and faulty connections in wiring, to waste electric current and reduce the power of electric motors.

(5) Damage to commutators can reduce the power output or cause short circuiting in direct-current motors: Loosen or remove commutator holding rings. Sprinkle carbon, graphite, or metal dust on commutators. Put a little grease or oil at the contact points of commutators. Where commutator bars are close together bridge the gaps between them with metal dust, or sawtooth their edges with a chisel so that the teeth on adjoining bars meet or nearly meet and current can pass from one to the other.

(6) Put a piece of finely grained emery paper half the size of a postage stamp in a place where it will wear away rotating brushes. The emery paper – and the motor – will be destroyed *in* the resulting fire.

(7) Sprinkle carbon, graphite or metal dust on slip-rings so that the current will leak or short circuits will occur. When a motor is idle, nick the slip-rings with a chisel.

(8) Cause motor stoppage or inefficiency by applying dust mixed with grease to the face of the armature so that it will not make proper contact.

(9) To overheat electric motors, mix sand with heavy grease and smear it between the stator and rotor, or wedge thin metal pieces between them. To prevent the efficient generation of current, put floor sweepings, oil, tar, or paint between them.

SLEEVE GUN

Catalogue No. N 254.

DESCRIPTION. Like the Sleeve Gun Mk. I the Mk. II is a short length, silent, murder weapon, firing 0·32 inch ammunition. It is a single shot weapon designed for carriage in the sleeve with the trigger near the muzzle to aid unobtrusive firing when the gun is slid from the sleeve into the hand. The gun is intended for use in contact with the target, but may be used at ranges up to about three yards; the silencing element cannot be removed for replacement since the gun is not intended for prolonged use.

The gun is fitted at the rear end with a ring to which the carrying lanyard can be attached.

In appearance the main difference between the Sleeve Gun Mks. I and II, is in the cocking tube of the Mk. I, which runs parallel to the main cylinder of the gun for its whole length; the depth of the weapon is thus near to its maximum value of 1¾ inches throughout the length of the gun. The Mk. II has no cocking tube and the only considerable protuberance from the main cylinder is the trigger; except for the foremost inch of the gun, the depth is therefore little more than the cylinder diameter of 1¼ inches. As a result, the Mk. II is a slimmer weapon than the Mk. I and much neater in appearance.

METHOD OF USE. The gun is carried up the sleeve until required, it is then slid into the hand and the muzzle pressed against the victim, at the same time operating the trigger with the thumb. After use, the gun returns to its position up the sleeve and all evidence such as the empty case is retained in the gun.

DIMENSIONS. Overall length 8¾". Diam. 1¼".   **WEIGHT.** 26 ozs.

S-PHONE

This completely portable ground station, complete with all batteries, is designed in the form of personal equipment, to be worn by the operator. Communication is between the ground station and a ship or aircraft, fitted with special equipment.

The transmitter-receiver, housed in a cast aluminium alloy case, is held in position on the operator's chest, by rings fitted to the shoulder straps, which support a cloth battery belt worn around the waist. Pockets in the belt are provided to contain the batteries and a vibrator power pack, which supply L.T. and H.T. current for the set.

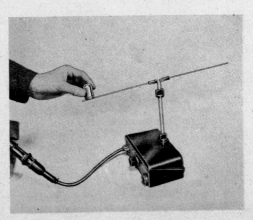

GENERAL DESCRIPTION.

Communication is carried as if over an ordinary telephone, speech quality is very similar, and as there is only one tuning control and one switch, any intelligent person is able to use the apparatus with the minimum of instruction.

Two valves are used in the transmitter, functioning as modulation (speech) amplifier and oscillator. No provision is made for adjusting the transmitter frequency, which is fixed to lie within the tuning range of the ship or plane receiver to which the ground station will transmit.

The receiver, a super-regenerative detector followed by a two-stage audio amplifier, employs three miniature valves. Receiver tuning can be adjusted by means of a knob located on the underside of the case.

A small collapsible aerial is provided which plugs into the front of the set.

The possibility of being overheard whilst transmitting is greatly reduced by the use of a microphone which restricts direct vocal radiation of the operator to within a few yards from where he is standing, when talking at a normal conversational level.

The microphone and headphone are attached to the transmitter-receiver by a flexible cable and a heavy-duty plug and socket. A similar plug and socket is used to link the battery belt and transmitter-receiver.

With the apparatus in position on the operator, it can be brought into operation merely by actuating a switch conveniently placed on the battery belt.

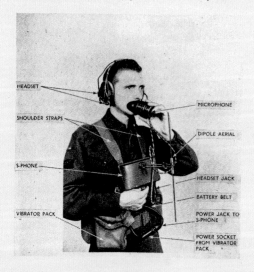

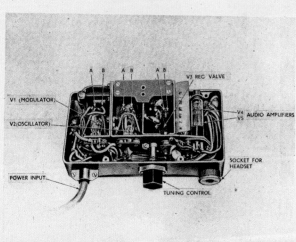

R.C.D. RECEIVER, TYPE 31/1 PROPAGANDA SET

GENERAL DESCRIPTION.

The R.C.D. type 31/1 is a pocket receiving set, employing three battery-operated miniature valves in a T.R.F. circuit. It is suitable for radio telephone and C.W. Morse reception, on the 25—50 metre band (6 to 12 Mcs.) The receiver and batteries (H.T.—L.T.) are housed in separate steel boxes, sprayed with grey crackle cellulose. The controls provided are "Tuning" and "Regeneration," the drum tuning scale being calibrated in metres. High and low tension supplies are connected when the receiver power cable is plugged into the correct socket on the battery box. The very sensitive telephones are of the miniature crystal deaf-aid type, which fit into the ear.

The receiver has been designed for operation in temperate or sub-tropical climates, primarily Western Europe, in which good reception should be obtainable from any of the short wave B.B.C. news transmitters. The mechanical construction is such as to ensure a high degree of durability.

DIMENSIONS AND WEIGHT.

	Length.	Width.	Depth.	Weight.
Receiver	5⅞"	4⅜"	1¹¹⁄₁₆"	1 lb. 2 ozs.
Battery unit (including H.T. and L.T. batteries)	4¼"	3¼"	1"	1 lb.

POWER SUPPLY.

Miniature 30 V. H.T. Dry Battery.   Standard 4.5 V. L.T. Dry Battery.

POWER CONSUMPTION.

H.T. 0.5 m.A.   L.T. 50 m.A.

BATTERY LIFE.

The H.T. and L.T. batteries will give useful service for 100 and 30 hours respectively, if used for a period not exceeding 1 hour and then given approximately the same interval of rest. Continuous operation will reduce these figures to 50—60 hours H.T. and 8 hours L.T. In temperate climates batteries should be put into service within 6 months from the date of manufacture. This period will be shorter in hot damp climates.

ACCESSORIES AND SPARES.

Miniature Crystal Telephones, wire for aerial and earth, 2 spare L.T. batteries and 1 spare H.T. battery are provided.

PACKING.

The crystal 'phones are sealed in a small tinned-steel container; this, together with all other items, including accessories and spares, are placed in cardboard wrappers, and then packed in a cardboard box. This method of packing is suitable for road and rail transport, and may be flown, provided the altitude does not exceed 15,000 ft.

When carried at higher altitudes, or transported by sea, it is essential that the cardboard box be placed in a tinned-steel container and hermetically sealed.

SIZE WHEN PACKED. 7½" x 5½" x 3".   **WEIGHT.** 3¾ lbs.

ARTICLES CARRIED BY A STUDENT

This section could very well be a catalogue in itself as even the many articles mentioned in the following pages do not in any way cover the whole field of material which comes under this heading.

Almost anything which a person carries or makes use of professionally, by way of trade, for personal convenience or toilet purposes, can be adapted for concealment.

This section covers all types of articles but by no means all varieties, and for simplicity it has been divided into sub-sections.

No. 1 sub-section deals with those concealments which are possible in the actual personal clothing and contents of the pockets of the average man.

PERSONAL ARTICLES.

The following is a short list of some of the articles which have been adapted:—

Collar stud
Collar stiffener
Coat button
Cigarette holder
Door key
Fountain pen
Finger ring
Pocket petrol lighter

Pocket torches
Pen knife
Pipe
Pipe cases
Pencils
Shoe trees
Shoulder paddings
Shoe heels and soles
Spectacles

The following examples show what can be done with these articles:—

Collar Stud. A metal collar stud with a celluloid back can be used for concealing micro prints. The celluloid back is removed, and the print placed in the cavity. The celluloid is replaced and secured with a small application of Seccotine.

Necktie. A necktie can conceal a small code printed on silk. The code is secured to the back of the tie with two small press studs. This method is used in order that the code may be very speedily used and replaced. A tie adapted in this manner is worn quite normally and without any bulkiness showing.

Door Key. A door key has been successfully adapted for the concealment of small microprints. The shaft of the key is drilled to about three quarters of its length, and a small stud is made which fits into the hollowed shaft by means of a left handed thread. See illustration.

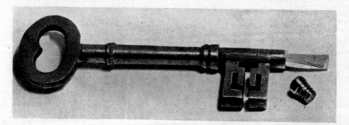

TOILET ARTICLES.

In the following list are some of the toilet articles which have been used for concealment purposes, and which form some of the personal equipment of a Student.

Bath salts.	Folding mirror.	Razor.	Manicure accessories.
Razor box.	Sponge.	Shaving soap.	Toilet soap.
Shaving stick.	Talcum powder.	Toilet roll.	Toothpaste.
Lipsticks.			

Examples from this list are given below.

Sponge. A suitable place in the sponge is chosen, and a hole is cut to conform to the natural texture of the sponge. A small amount of the sponge fibre is cut away from the inside to leave sufficient room to insert a message or code printed on silk. The object inserted in a sponge must necessarily be of a soft nature in order not to make a hard lump and to avoid a rustling sound which would be made by paper.

The cavity in the sponge is closed up by replacing a small sponge plug and securing with Seccotine or by stitching.

Toilet Soap. It is necessary to procure or copy a cake of soap common to the district where the Student is proceeding.

The piece of soap is carefully split open and the centre hollowed out. Pins are used to help to keep the two halves together. When the object for concealment is in place, the soap is pressed together. To render the joint unnoticeable a little moisture is rubbed round the joint, or the soap is used in the normal way.

Toothpaste in Tubes. These tubes have a number of uses. The Student naturally requires toothpaste appropriate to the country to which he is proceeding. Some of the "brands" which are made up by the Camouflage Section are shown below. Glass-frosting ointment is also dispatched under this cover.

For concealment purposes the tubes are completed with the supposed makers' trade marks, etc., and the top of the tube is filled with toothpaste. If the object to be concealed requires to be damp-proofed (e.g. a code printed on silk), it is inserted in a rubber balloon. The object is placed in the tube, packed with a little cotton wool

and the end of the tube is folded over in the normal way. This device is safe enough because the toothpaste can be used and should arouse no suspicion.

Shaving Cream in Tubes. This method is exactly similar to the toothpaste tube, except that there is a larger concealment space. Examples are shown.

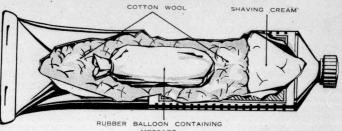

COTTON WOOL   SHAVING CREAM

RUBBER BALLOON CONTAINING MESSAGE

BRUSHES.

The following is a list of some of the brushes used for concealment:—

Hair brushes, celluloid backs, wooden backs, and swivel sided. Shaving brushes. Clothes brushes. Tooth brushes. Nail brushes. Shoe brushes. Paint and distemper brushes. Wire brushes.

These are used for concealment of codes, money, documents, etc. There are two principal methods used for brushes. When the brush is used to carry money, etc. to the field and is not re-used, the back of a celluloid brush, for example, is removed, money is packed inside the cavity, and the brush sealed up. The brush must be split open to extract its contents. If the brush is for use on a number of occasions the swivel sided brush described on the next page is an example of the type of brush supplied.

The following are some descriptions of typical brush concealments.

Celluloid Hair brush and Shaving brush. In the illustration below is shown a complete toilet set in a leather case. The case itself has a concealment pocket and the

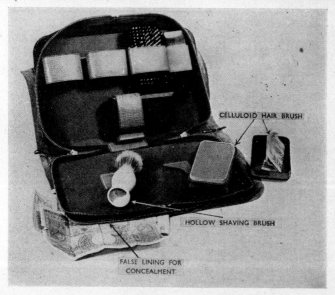

CELLULOID HAIR BRUSH

HOLLOW SHAVING BRUSH

FALSE LINING FOR CONCEALMENT

hair brush is of the celluloid back type. The shaving brush is hollow as shown. These three devices are for use only once each, because each article must be forcibly opened to extract the hidden contents.

Swivel type Hair brush. The photograph shows the working of the swivel sided hair brush. The cavity is approximately 3 inches x 2 inches x ⅜ inch.

Shaving brush. This brush is also for quick and frequent use. The bristles are held in place by a tight metal ring which clamps them to the handle. This brush must not be confused with the type, shown in the illustration on the previous page, which can only be used once.

Tooth brush. A celluloid handled tooth brush can be used for concealment of small micro prints. The handle of the brush is drilled, the print inserted and the hole sealed by softening the celluloid with acetone and smoothing off on a buffing wheel. To extract the message the handle of the brush must be broken.

Various types of Leather Goods can be used for the concealment of Codes, Money, Documents, etc. A list of these is given below.

LEATHER GOODS.

1. Brief cases.
2. Cycle Saddle bag.
3. Cigarette cases.
4. Card cases.
5. Handbags, ladies'.
6. Needle cases and housewives.
7. Pocket chess set.
8. Razor strop.
9. Suit cases, various types.
10. Tobacco pouches.
11. Pocket note books, various types.
12. Toilet cases, various types.
13. Wallets, Photo and Money.
14. Writing cases, various types.
15. Leather belts and braces.
16. Hairbrush case.
17. Toolbags.

Two methods are used in the camouflage of Codes, Documents, etc.

1. Where the article is used only once for transporting Money and Documents to the Field, it can be sealed and ripped open when needed.
2. In the case of Codes when the article would have to be used many times, a concealed flap device is incorporated in the design so that the Code can be readily accessible.

Brief Cases. These are of Continental design in various sizes and colours, having double sided partitions, with fake sewing along the top. Partitions are glued together after the Documents have been inserted.

(10) In motors using three-phase current, deeply nick one of the lead-in wires with a knife or file when the machine is at rest, or replace one of the three fuses with a blown-out fuse. In the first case, the motor will stop after running awhile, and in the second, it will not start.

(f) Transformers

(1) Transformers of the oil-filled type can be put out of commission if you pour water, salt water, coolant, or kerosene into the oil tank.

(2) In air-cooled transformers, block the ventilation by piling debris around the transformer.

(3) In all types of transformers, throw carbon, graphite or metal dust over the outside bushings and other exposed electrical parts.

(g) Turbines for the most part are heavily built, stoutly housed, and difficult of access. Their vulnerability to simple sabotage is very low.

(1) After inspecting or repairing a hydro turbine, fasten the cover insecurely so that it will blow off and flood the plant with water. A loose cover on a steam turbine will cause it to leak and slow down.

(2) In water turbines, insert a large piece of scrap iron in the head of the penstock, just beyond the screening, so that water will carry the damaging material down to the plant equipment.

(3) When the steam line to a turbine is opened for repair, put pieces of scrap iron into it, to be blasted into the turbine machinery when steam is up again.

(4) Create a leak in the line feeding oil to the turbine, so that oil will fall on the hot steam pipe and cause a fire.

(h) Boilers

(1) Reduce the efficiency of steam boilers any way you can. Put too much water in them to make them slow-starting, or keep the fire under them low to keep them inefficient. Let them dry and turn the fire up; they will crack and be ruined. An especially good trick is to keep putting limestone or water containing lime in the boiler; it will deposit lime on the bottom and sides. This deposit will provide very good insulation against heat; after enough of it has collected, the boiler will be completely worthless.

(3) Production Metals

(a) Iron and Steel

(1) Keep blast furnaces in a condition where they must be frequently shut down for repair. In making fire-proof bricks for the inner lining of blast furnaces, put in an extra proportion of tar so that they will wear out quickly and necessitate constant re-lining.

(2) Make cores for casting so that they are filled with air bubbles and an imperfect cast results.

(3) See that the core in a mold is not properly supported, so that the core gives way or the casting is spoiled because of the incorrect position of the core.

(4) In tempering steel or iron, apply too much heat, so that the resulting bars and ingots are of poor quality.

(b) Other Metals

No suggestions available.

(4) Production: Mining and Mineral Extraction

(a) Coal

(1) A slight blow against your Davy oil lamp will extinguish it, and to light it again you will have to find a place where there is no fire damp. Take a long time looking for the place.

(2) Blacksmiths who make pneumatic picks should not harden them properly, so that they will quickly grow dull.

(3) You can easily put your pneumatic pick out of order. Pour a small amount of water through the oil lever and your pick will stop working. Coal dust and improper lubrication will also put it out of order.

(4) Weaken the chain that pulls the bucket conveyers carrying coal. A deep dent in the chain made with blows of a pick or shovel will cause it to part under normal strain. Once a chain breaks, normally or otherwise, take your time about reporting the damage; be slow about taking the chain up for repairs and bringing it back down after repairs.

(5) Derail mine cars by putting obstructions on the rails and in switch points. If possible, pick a gallery where coal cars have to pass each other, so that traffic will be snarled up.

(6) Send up quantities of rock and other useless material with the coal.

(5) Production: Agriculture

(a) Machinery

(1) See par. 5 b. (2) (c), (d) and (e).

(b) Crops and livestock probably will be destroyed only in areas where there are large food surpluses or where the enemy (regime) is known to be requisitioning food.

(1) Feed crops to livestock. Let crops harvest too early or too late. Spoil stores of grain, fruit and vegetables by soaking them in water so that they will rot. Spoil fruit and vegetables by leaving them in the sun.

(6) Transportation: Railways

(a) Passengers

(1) Make train travel as inconvenient as possible for enemy personnel. Make mistakes in issuing train tickets, leaving portions of the journey uncovered by the ticket book; issue two tickets for the same seat in the train, so that an interesting argument will result; near train time, instead of issuing printed tickets write them out slowly by hand, prolonging the process until the train is nearly ready to leave or has left the station. On station bulletin boards announcing train arrivals and departures, see that false and misleading information is given about trains bound for enemy destinations.

(2) In trains bound for enemy destinations, attendants should make life as uncomfortable as possible for passengers. See that the food is especially bad, take up tickets after midnight, call all station stops very loudly during the night, handle baggage as noisily as possible during the night, and so on.

(3) See that the luggage of enemy personnel is mislaid or unloaded at the wrong stations. Switch address labels on enemy baggage.

(4) Engineers should see that trains run slow or make unscheduled stops for plausible reasons.

(b) Switches, Signals and Routing

(1) Exchange wires in switchboards containing signals and switches, so that they connect to the wrong terminals.

(2) Loosen push-rods so that signal arms do not work; break signal lights; exchange the colored lenses on red and green lights.

(3) Spread and spike switch points in the track so that they will not move, or place rocks or close-packed dirt between the switch points.

(4) Sprinkle rock salt or ordinary salt profusely over the electrical connections of switch points and on the ground nearby. When it rains, the switch will be short-circuited.

(5) See that cars are put on the wrong trains. Remove the labels from cars needing repair and put them on cars in good order. Leave couplings between cars as loose as possible.

(c) Road-beds and Open Track

(1) On a curve, take the bolts out of the tie-plates connecting to sections of the outside rail, and scoop away the gravel, cinders, or dirt for a few feet on each side of the connecting joint.

(2) If by disconnecting the tie-plate at a joint and loosening

sleeper nails on each side of the joint, it becomes possible to move a section of rail, spread two sections of rail and drive a spike vertically between them.

(d) Oil and Lubrication

(1) See 5 b. (2) (b).

(2) Squeeze lubricating pipes with pincers or dent them with hammers, so that the flow of oil is obstructed.

(e) Cooling Systems

(1) See 5 b. (2) (c).

(f) Gasoline and Oil Fuel

(1) See 5 b. (2) (d).

(g) Electric Motors

(1) See 5 b. (2) (e) and (f).

(h) Boilers

(1) See 5 b. (2) (h).

(2) After inspection put heavy oil or tar in the engines' boilers, or put half a kilogram of soft soap into the water in the tender.

(i) Brakes and Miscellaneous

(1) Engines should run at high speeds and use brakes excessively at curves and on downhill grades.

(2) Punch holes in air-brake valves or water supply pipes.

(3) In the last car of a passenger train or the front car of a freight, remove the wadding from a journal box and replace it with oily rags.

(7) Transportation: Automotive

(a) **Roads**

Damage to roads [(3) below] is slow, and therefore impractical as a D-day or near D-day activity.

(1) Change sign posts at intersections and forks; the enemy will go the wrong way and it may be miles before he discovers his mistakes. In areas where traffic is composed primarily of enemy autos, trucks, and motor convoys of various kinds, remove danger signals from curves and intersections.

(2) When the enemy asks for directions, give him wrong information. Especially when enemy convoys are in the neighborhood, truck drivers can spread rumors and give false information about bridges being out, ferries closed, and detours lying ahead.

(3) If you can start damage to a heavily traveled road, passing traffic and the elements will do the rest. Construction gangs can see that too much sand or water is put in concrete or that the road foundation has soft spots. Anyone can scoop ruts in asphalt and macadam roads which turn soft in hot weather; passing trucks will accentuate the ruts to a point where substantial repair will be needed. Dirt roads also can be scooped out. If you are a road laborer, it will be only a few minutes work to divert a small stream from a sluice so

that it runs over and eats away the road.

(4) Distribute broken glass, nails, and sharp rocks on roads to puncture tires.

(b) Passengers

(1) Bus-drivers can go past the stop where the enemy wants to get off. Taxi drivers can waste the enemy's time and make extra money by driving the longest possible route to his destination.

(c) Oil and Lubrication

(1) See 5 b. (2) (b).

(2) Disconnect the oil pump; this will burn out the main bearings in less than 50 miles of normal driving.

(d) Radiator

(1) See 5 b. (2) (c).

(e) Fuel

(1) See 5 b. (2) (d).

(f) Battery and Ignition

(1) Jam bits of wood into the ignition lock; loosen or exchange connections behind the switchboard; put dirt in spark plugs; damage distributor points.

(2) Turn on the lights in parked cars so that the battery will run down.

(3) Mechanics can ruin batteries in a number of undetectable ways: Take the valve cap off a cell, and drive a screw driver slantwise into the exposed water vent, shattering the plates of the cell; no damage will show when you put the cap back on. Iron or copper filings put into the cells i.e., dropped into the acid, will greatly shorten its life. Copper coins or a few pieces of iron will accomplish the same and more slowly. One hundred to 150 cubic centimeters of vinegar in each cell greatly reduces the life of the battery, but the odor of the vinegar may reveal what has happened.

(g) Gears

(1) Remove the lubricant from or put too light a lubricant in the transmission and other gears.

(2) In trucks, tractors, and other machines with heavy gears, fix the gear case insecurely, putting bolts in only half the bolt holes. The gears will be badly jolted in use and will soon need repairs.

(h) Tires

(1) Slash or puncture tires of unguarded vehicles. Put a nail inside a match box or other small box, and set it vertically in front of the back tire of a stationary car; when the car starts off, the nail will go neatly through the tire.

(2) It is easy to damage a tire in a tire repair shop: In fixing flats, spill glass, benzine, caustic soda, or other material inside the casing which will puncture or corrode the tube. If you put a gummy substance inside the tube, the next flat will stick the tube to the casing and make it unusable. Or, when you fix a flat tire, you can simply leave between the tube and the casing the object which caused the flat in the first place.

(3) In assembling a tire after repair, pump the tube up as fast as you can. Instead of filling out smoothly, it may crease, in which case it will wear out quickly. Or, as you put a tire together, see if you can pinch the tube between the rim of the tire and the rim of the wheel, so that a blow-out will result.

(4) In putting air into tires, see that they are kept below normal pressure, so that more than an ordinary amount of wear will result. In filling tires on double wheels, inflate the inner tire to a much higher pressure than the outer one; both will wear out more quickly this way. Badly aligned wheels also wear tires out quickly; you can leave wheels out of alignment when they come in for adjustment, or you can spring them out of true with a strong kick, or by driving the car slowly and diagonally into a curb.

(5) If you have access to stocks of tires, you can rot them by spilling oil, gasoline, caustic acid, or benzine on them. Synthetic rubber, however, is less susceptible to these chemicals.

(8) Transportation: Water

(a) Navigation

(1) Barge and river boat personnel should spread false rumors about the navigability and conditions of the waterways they travel. Tell other barge and boat captains to follow channels that will take extra time, or cause them to make canal detours.

(2) Barge and river boat captains should navigate with exceeding caution near locks and bridges, to waste their time and to waste the time of other craft which may have to wait on them. If you don't pump the bilges of ships and barges often enough, they will be slower and harder to navigate: Barges "accidently" run aground are an efficient time waster too.

(3) Attendants on swing, draw, or bascule bridges can delay traffic over the bridge or in the waterway underneath by being slow. Boat captains can leave unattended draw bridges open in order to hold up road traffic.

(4) Add or subtract compensating magnets to the compass on cargo ships. Demagnetize the compass or maladjust it by concealing a large bar of steel or iron near to it.

(b) Cargo

(1) While loading or unloading, handle cargo carelessly in order to cause damage. Arrange the cargo so that the weakest and lightest crates and boxes will be at the bottom of the hold, while the heaviest ones are on top of them. Put hatch covers and tarpaulins on sloppily, so that rain and deck wash will injure the cargo. Tie float valves open so that storage tanks will overflow on perishable goods.

(9) Communications

(a) Telephone

(1) At office, hotel and exchange switchboards delay putting enemy calls through, give them wrong numbers, cut them off "accidentally," or forget to disconnect them so that the line cannot be used again.

(2) Hamper official and especially military business by making at least one telephone call a day to an enemy headquarters; when you get them, tell them you have the wrong number. Call military or police offices and make anonymous false reports of fires, air raids, bombs.

(3) In offices and buildings used by the enemy, unscrew the

earphone of telephone receivers and remove the diaphragm. Electricians and telephone repair men can make poor connections and damage insulation so that cross-talk and other kinds of electrical interference will make conversations hard or impossible to understand.

(4) Put the batteries under automatic switchboards out of commission by dropping nails, metal filings, or coins into the cells. If you can treat half the batteries in this way, the switchboard will stop working. A whole telephone system can be disrupted if you can put 10 percent of the cells in half the batteries of the central battery room out of order.

(b) Telegraph

(1) Delay the transmission and delivery of telegrams to enemy destinations.

(2) Garble telegrams to enemy destinations so that another telegram will have to be sent or a long distance call will have to be made. Sometimes it will be possible to do this by changing a single letter in a word – for example, changing "minimum" to "miximum," so that the person receiving the telegram will not know whether "minimum" or "maximum" is meant.

(c) Transportation Lines

(1) Cut telephone and telegraph transmission lines. Damage insulation on power lines to cause interference.

(d) Mail

(1) Post office employees can see to it that enemy mail is always delayed by one day or more, that it is put in wrong sacks, and so on.

(e) Motion Pictures

(1) Projector operators can ruin newsreels and other enemy propaganda films by bad focusing, speeding up or slowing down the film and by causing frequent breakage in the film.

(2) Audiences can ruin enemy propaganda films by applauding to drown the words of the speaker, by coughing loudly, and by talking.

(3) Anyone can break up a showing of an enemy propaganda film by putting two or three dozen large moths in a paper bag. Take the bag to the movies with you, put it on the floor in an empty section of the theater as you go in and leave it open. The moths will fly out and climb into the projector beam, so that the film will be obscured by fluttering shadows.

(f) Radio

(1) Station engineers will find it quite easy to overmodulate transmissions of talks by persons giving enemy propaganda or instructions, so that they will sound as if they were talking through a heavy cotton blanket with a mouth full of marbles.

(2) In your own apartment building, you can interfere with radio reception at times when the enemy wants everybody to listen. Take an electric light plug off the end of an electric light cord; take some wire out of the cord and tie it across two terminals of a two-prong plug or three terminals of a four-prong plug. Then take it around and put it into as many wall and floor outlets as you can find. Each time you insert the plug into a new circuit, you will blow out a fuse and silence all radios running on power from that circuit until a new fuse is put in.

(3) Damaging insulation on any electrical equipment tends to create radio interference in the immediate neighborhood, particularly on large generators, neon signs, fluorescent lighting, X-ray machines, and power lines. If workmen can damage insulation on a high tension line near an enemy airfield, they will make ground-to-plane radio communications difficult and perhaps impossible during long periods of the day.

(10) Electric Power

(a) Turbines, Electric Motors, Transformers

(b) (1) See 5 b. (2) (e), (f), and (g).

(c) Transmission Lines

(1) Linesmen can loosen and dirty insulators to cause power leakage. It will be quite easy, too, for them to tie a piece of very heavy string several times back and forth between two parallel transmission lines, winding it several turns around the wire each time. Beforehand, the string should be heavily saturated with salt and then dried. When it rains, the string becomes a conductor, and a short-circuit will result.

(11) General Interference with Organizations and Production

(a) Organizations and Conferences

(1) Insist on doing everything through "channels." Never permit short-cuts to be taken in order to expedite decisions.

(2) Make "speeches." Talk as frequently as possible and at great length. Illustrate your "points" by long anecdotes and

accounts of personal experiences. Never hesitate to make a few appropriate "patriotic" comments.

(3) When possible, refer all matters to committees, for "further study and consideration." Attempt to make the committees as large as possible – never less than five.

(4) Bring up irrelevant issues as frequently as possible.

(5) Haggle over precise wordings of communications, minutes, resolutions.

(6) Refer back to matters decided upon at the last meeting and attempt to re-open the question of the advisability of that decision.

(7) Advocate "caution." Be "reasonable" and urge your fellow-conferees to be "reasonable" and avoid haste which might result in embarrassments or difficulties later on.

(8) Be worried about the propriety of any decision – raise the question of whether such action as is contemplated lies within the jurisdiction of the group or whether it might conflict with the policy of some higher echelon.

(b) Managers and Supervisors

(1) Demand written orders.

(2) "Misunderstand" orders. Ask endless questions or engage in long correspondence about such orders. Quibble over them when you can.

(3) Do everything possible to delay the delivery of orders. Even though parts of an order may be ready beforehand,

don't deliver it until it is completely ready.

(4) Don't order new working materials until your current stocks have been virtually exhausted, so that the slightest delay in filling your order will mean a shutdown.

(5) Order high-quality materials which are hard to get. If you don't get them argue about it. Warn that inferior materials will mean inferior work.

(6) In making work assignments, always sign out the unimportant jobs first. See that the important jobs are assigned to inefficient workers of poor machines.

(7) Insist on perfect work in relatively unimportant products; send back for refinishing those which have the least flaw. Approve other defective parts whose flaws are not visible to the naked eye.

(8) Make mistakes in routing so that parts and materials will be sent to the wrong place in the plant.

(9) When training new workers, give incomplete or misleading instructions.

(10) To lower morale and with it, production, be pleasant to inefficient workers; give them undeserved promotions. Discriminate against efficient workers; complain unjustly about their work.

(11) Hold conferences when there is more critical work to be done.

(12) Multiply paper work in plausible ways. Start duplicate files.

(13) Multiply the procedures and clearances involved in issuing instructions, pay checks, and so on. See that three people have to approve everything where one would do.

(14) Apply all regulations to the last letter.

(c) Office Workers

(1) Make mistakes in quantities of material when you are copying orders. Confuse similar names. Use wrong addresses.

(2) Prolong correspondence with government bureaus.

(3) Misfile essential documents.

(4) In making carbon copies, make one too few, so that an extra copying job will have to be done.

(5) Tell important callers the boss is busy or talking on another telephone.

(6) Hold up mail until the next collection.

(7) Spread disturbing rumors that sound like inside dope.

(d) Employees

(1) *Work slowly.* Think out ways to increase the number of movements necessary on your job: use a light hammer instead of a heavy one, try to make a small wrench do when a big one is necessary, use little force where considerable force is needed, and so on.

(2) Contrive as many interruptions to your work as you can:

when changing the material on which you are working, as
you would on a lathe or punch, take needless time to do it. If
you are cutting, shaping or doing other measured work,
measure dimensions twice as often as you need to. When you
go to the lavatory, spend a longer time there than is necessary.
Forget tools so that you will have to go back after them.

(3) Even if you understand the language, pretend not to
understand instructions in a foreign tongue.

(4) Pretend that instructions are hard to understand, and ask to
have them repeated more than once. Or pretend that you
are particularly anxious to do your work, and pester the
foreman with unnecessary questions.

(5) Do your work poorly and blame it on bad tools, machinery,
or equipment. Complain that these things are preventing
you from doing your job right.

(6) Never pass on your skill and experience to a new or less
skillful worker.

(7) Snarl up administration in every possible way. Fill out forms
illegibly so that they will have to be done over; make
mistakes or omit requested information in forms.

(8) If possible, join or help organize a group for presenting
employee problems to the management. See that the
procedures adopted are as inconvenient as possible for the
management, involving the presence of a large number of
employees at each presentation, entailing more than one
meeting for each grievance, bringing up problems which
are largely imaginary, and so on.

(9) Misroute materials.

(10) Mix good parts with unusable scrap and rejected parts.

(12) General Devices for Lowering Morale and Creating Confusion

(a) Give lengthy, incomprehensible explanations when questioned.

(b) Report imaginary spies or danger to the Gestapo or police.

(c) Act stupid.

(d) Be as irritable and quarrelsome as possible without getting yourself into trouble.

(e) Misunderstand all sorts of regulations concerning such matters as rationing, transportation, traffic regulations.

(f) Complain against ersatz materials.

(g) In public treat axis nationals or quislings coldly.

(h) Stop all conversation when axis nationals or quislings enter a cafe.

(i) Cry and sob hysterically at every occasion, especially when confronted by government clerks.

(j) Boycott all movies, entertainments, concerts, newspapers which are in any way connected with the quisling authorities.

(k) Do not cooperate in salvage schemes.

MANUAL OF DISGUISE, 1944

OSS

Appearing to be anything but secret agent was a key part of the training and equipment of the SOE and OSS. Early mistakes included sending personnel into occupied countries wearing inappropriate dress, or with documents supposedly from different organisations issued on different dates containing similar handwriting. The extracts from the OSS manual reproduced here make telling points about blending in, and recommends the employment of simple devices that can easily be adopted in the field. Generally such techniques were learned with the help of experts in the training school, but as far as possible all evidence of their application was left behind when operatives applied them in occupied territory. In the most extreme cases a few agents who were particularly recognisable were given plastic surgery – George Langelaan, for example, was given a reshaped chin and ears.

SOE literature provided lists of typical clothing and personal items for agents, and special extras for those 'proceeding to join the Maquis', including rucksacks, berets and ski caps. While large stocks of men's clothes were held, women's' attire was given more individual attention on each mission due to the greater regional and seasonal variation. Garments were made specially and 'aged', or obtained second-hand from refugees. The wardrobe staff of SOE issued almost 9,000 pieces of clothing during a single month in 1944. The most exotic productions were enemy uniforms, complete with bullion thread insignia counterfeited in a Preston workshop.

MI9 and the US Army's 'Military Intelligence Section Escape and Evasion' also had a special interest in disguise, as well as forgery and concealed navigation aids, for use in escapes. In the case of prisoners of war, however, still greater improvisation had to be the order of the day. Clothes had to be converted or dyed, silk maps and miniature compasses hidden. Documents were stolen to order, or copied using such ingenious devices as 'lifting' signatures with boiled eggs.

TEMPORARY DISGUISE

Temporary disguise may be considered in two phases:

(a) Quick Changes. These enable you, through your own ingenuity, and using mainly materials at hand, to throw a "shadow" off your trail, for example, or to get through a spot check.

(b) *Prepared* Quick Changes. These serve the same purpose as quick changes but have this advantage: nothing needs to be rounded up at the last minute. Your change has been carefully worked out in advance for the best quick effect possible. You have practiced with it and acquired speed in its application, and you have been provided with all the necessary articles, carefully concealed, before you leave your base.

Quick Changes

Without knowing the individual problem presented, only suggestions and helpful hints can be offered. The type of clothes you will be wearing will determine, to some degree, the amount of change you can make. It will be much easier to switch from a bank clerk to a tramp, for example, than vice versa. Consider also the district you have to pass through in making your escape. If it is the wharves, you will be less noticeable as a seaman, a truck driver or a stevedore. If it is a financial district, become the most typical of clerks. Remember, even when changing your disguise, you must still be one of the crowd.

It is up to you as a student to try out various combinations and see for yourself the often surprising changes that can be made quickly. You will find that one idea will suggest another. Work with another student at first, then by yourself, and *time* yourself. If possible, get into your complete cover clothes, stand before a mirror, study every detail of your appearance and ask yourself, "What can I do most quickly to change that man?" Then go to work.

(1) Shape of Body

To make yourself taller, two or two and a half inches can be quickly added to your height by tearing or folding a newspaper to form a ramp in the heels of your shoes. If you are wearing high top shoes, even more can be added. Be certain that you replace them tightly and tie a double knot. Such ramps have an added advantage in that they also change your walk and posture. Practice walking with them, though, or you will find yourself tip-toeing rather than putting your heel down first as is normal.

Restyle the crown of your hat, using its complete height. (Remember the pictures of Lincoln in his plug hat? Although he was very tall himself, his hat made him appear to tower over others.) The narrower the brim of the hat the better. If an overcoat is worn, it should preferably be a short one showing a length of legs below it. A short cane, stick or small-sized umbrella will contribute to the illusion of height.

Hoist your trousers way up and tighten the belt. This will make your legs look longer. Excessive padding in the shoulders should be removed to narrow your frame. Side pockets should be emptied. If wearing a single breasted coat, leave it open or button it at the bottom button. Undo your vest, showing as much length of tie as you can. Pull your collar down showing as much neck as you can.

In other words, everything about you should be on the vertical, thin line, while your "props" should be narrow but undersized for comparison. Finally, *stand up straight*.

To appear shorter, the reverse of everything above should be done. Flatten your hat; the wider the brim the better. Slump down and bend your knees a bit. Let a double breasted coat hang open. Stuff the side pockets. Button a single breasted suit to the top. Push your trousers way down so that they bag around the ankles and the crotch is lower to make your legs look shorter. If you are wearing suspenders, let them out. Towels, rags or paper, properly shaped, can be put under your shirt in the front of your shorts to form a pot belly; the shorts will help hold them. Leave the bottom buttons of your vest open, showing an inverted V of shirt. Top trouser buttons need not be buttoned. Let our your belt a few notches and arc it down. Widen your coat shoulders by padding. With help, a towel or vest can be used to round the shoulders or back if made smooth and secured well. Hunch the coat and your collar up on your neck. A bow tie is best, but if a long tie is worn, show as little of it as possible.

Hand props should be of the bulky variety and care should be taken to carry them the way they are normally carried in the district. Many articles, for example, even steamer trunks and pianos, are carried on the head in many parts of the world.

To sum up: for the "short" effect, keep everything on the horizontal, wide plane. Use bulky, correct props for cover and carry them in the right way.

(2) Face, Hair and Hands

Pick out your most prominent features. These are the ones to disguise. Wads of cotton or paper between the teeth and under the cheeks will change a thin face to a fuller one. A roll of cotton or paper under the upper lip or the lower, or both, will radically change the profile.

If you are wearing a mustache, every attempt should be made to remove it, or to at least cut it down to a stubble so that it loses its previous character. If you do not have a mustache, it is possible to make one on the spot in a few minutes, using your own body hair (the hair of the head is usually too greasy to stick), *provided* you have taken the trouble to practice beforehand, and carry with you a small vial of liquid adhesive or spirit gum. These you can get from your base make-up kit. A very sharp knife, razor blade or a pair of nail scissors will also be needed to cut and trim the hair. Detailed instructions will be found in Chapter II [not included here].

A note of caution: Self-made mustaches at best will not stand too close a scrutiny in the daytime. In dim light or at night, however, they serve very well. Their main advantages are that they appear to change one's age; they hide or distract from a noticeable mouth or lips; they make a prominent nose seem smaller; and they effectively change a distinctive profile.

If you have a pair of glasses and were not wearing them before, put them on. If you were wearing them for your first cover, remove them for your second. (Consult a mirror to make sure you are not overdoing your effects: one can often be found in men's lavatories.)

A good swarthy or dirty skin color can be had by wetting your hands and rubbing them on an old piece of rusty iron. The fume-vent of a water heater is often a good place to find it. If sandpaper or emery cloth is available, you can obtain the coloring more quickly: otherwise, if the surface is hard, scrape it with your knife.

It is best to wash your face first, for the coloring tends to cake up if the skin surface is greasy. Leave your face damp and rub on the rust with both hands with a washing motion, using enough water but not too much. If the face is too wet, dry it off and start again. If the color from the rust streaks, dampen it a bit and work over it quickly. A smooth effect can be obtained. Great care should be exercised to cover completely all skin showing – inside the ears, behind the ears, the back of the neck, into the hair-line, the hair parting, the nostrils, the eye lids. Don't leave any white spots that will give you away. When the coloring is dry, brush off the larger specks.

Soot from inside a water heater or almost any stove pipe can be used to darken the eyebrows and the hair. With careful use of soot, coal dust, charcoal, charred wood, burned matches, black ashes of paper, a burned cork or even shoeblack, the eyes can be faintly shadowed on the top and bottom lids to add to the swarthy effect. Be careful not to overdo the effect and to blend all edges out to nothing. Try using a little of the black mixed with the rust color to accentuate "bags" under the eyes, hollows in cheeks or even a broken nose effect, which is achieved by adding faint shadows high on one side of the nose and near the tip on the other side, and rubbing the color off on the opposite side, so that your own lighter skin forms a highlight. Cheek bones can be heightened in the same way.

The sharp point of a burned match can serve as a pencil to

thicken eyebrows. *Draw* hairs on the brow rather than smudge them on. Try drawing a few hairs on the nose bridge and note the "heavy" effect. Applying shadows high on both sides of the bridge of the nose adds age.

A mechanic's face, with ingrained grease, can be affected by rubbing in black grease from an engine or hub-cap, or even plain soot in a drop or two of oil, and then rubbing some of it off. A fine crop of synthetic blackheads can also be achieved this way. Shoeblack rubbed very thin on the face gives a gray, unhealthy, almost dead look to the skin.

Shoeblack brushed into the nap of clothes, hats, caps, around the collar, etc., and a damp soap bar rubbed into that, give a good imitation of shiny, crusted dirt and grease. It should be done while the clothes are naturally wrinkled to the body, since the top of wrinkles catch most of the dirt.

Try the following effects for greying hair, mustache or eyebrows. The results will vary with the materials as well as with the texture and greasiness of the student's hair. Try grey ashes, both wood and paper, powdered down by rubbing them in the palm of the hand; try talcum powder, flour or shoe-white greyed down a bit with one of the blacks. Comb this in well and add more until you get the effect you want. Try not to get it on the skin at the hair line or in the thin hair above the ears or back of the head. If you do, remove it. When you have succeeded in making the body of the hair grey, take some of the whitest hair in one palm, rub the hands together, and go over the area lightly, just touching the top hairs. Comb it carefully or rumple it up to fit the character you are assuming.

The effect of a stubble beard of one or two days' growth is best put on by using a dark thick grease and a rough sponge; certain brushes or a coarse napped material will serve. Stipple or pat the grease on the natural beard area, being careful not to make it too dark or heavy. Try for evenness and thin it out on the top edges.

Don't forget the hands. They too must match. Treat them with the same coloring as the face and to the same degree. Check up on your nails. Should they be clean or dirty?

Remember, if you are not too sure of some effect, use it only at night. In the daytime use only the few selected, simple, most effective disguises you are sure of from practice and know you have time to complete. Time yourself. Wear the effects and time *them* to see how long you can count on each one.

(3) Posture and Gait

If you have round shoulders, a strong "figure eight" cord, crossed in the back, will serve as a reminder to throw out your chest and stand up straight. Put your arms through it and slip it over your head. If you *want* round shoulders, cross it in front. Tying your suspenders together high up in the back will do the same thing to a lesser extent.

Try the old trick of buttoning your pants to your vest to acquire a stoop. Another way to keep hunched over is to use a strip of adhesive plaster stuck from just above the navel up to the hair on the chest. It should be applied while slouched over. Then try to straighten up!

Basically, posture and gait must fit the type of man you are portraying, his age, upbringing, physical condition, degree of ambition, and his whole outlook on life. Even without making a clothes change, a student can assume a completely different cover merely by changing his gait and switching to the exact opposite of the tempo used in the first cover.

Start now to observe how men of different classes of society and age sit, stand and walk. One section of the crowd will move with a purpose, preoccupied with their own important little lives. Another group will slouch or waddle along, like dully curious animals. Any little object catches their interest for a fleeting moment. They have no goal in life and every movement and line of their body show it.

Building up the inside of one shoe-heel will give a "short-leg" limp. With the same device it is easy to assume the walk of someone who has been paralyzed on one side. Build up, say, your left heel about an inch and a half, crook your right arm into a useless set, drop the right shoulder down and *swing* the right half-dead leg forward. Be sure your face has that drooped, dull, set expression of one who has had a stroke. The eyes are usually all that move, with a bewildered, anxious expression as though the person does not quite know what has happened to him. This cover, if not overplayed, has a good psychological angle because one's natural impulse is to look away from such cripples.

A small stone or other hard object in one sock heel will produce a convincing limp. Slightly larger ones in the arch of each foot will produce a "flat foot" walk. Detachable rubber pencil erasers or other firm but pliable articles are best for this because they do not bruise the foot so much over a period of time. Putting them inside the sock helps keep them in place. The last-mentioned device also aids in maintaining an "old age" gait. Try also a tight bandage around the calf of your leg with something under it to hurt the muscle as the weight is put on that foot.

Try the "lost arm", which is best done when wearing a double-breasted coat. Take the left arm from the coat sleeve. Tuck the empty sleeve in the coat pocket. Hold the elbow close to the waist at the side front and put your forearm around your waist with the left hand resting on the right hip. If you can button your vest around your arm, it will keep it even flatter, but you may want your arm more readily available. The other arrangement can be very convincing provided your coat is not too tight.

(4) Props or Accessories

Props or accessories have been mentioned above but their importance should be stressed again. Certain props definitely reflect a man's personality, and for our purpose can help give him personality. This is particularly true of smoking. A pipe usually indicates a certain type of man, as does a cigar. (Cigars, however, may be unobtainable in your district, or be so rare as to excite notice.) Different types of cigarettes and the many ways of handling them are also a surprisingly good key to their user. Study the people around you and this will become increasingly evident. Study yourself, also, to see if you have developed peculiar habits in smoking that might be noticed. If so, get rid of them.

Brief cases, bundles and their wrappings, lodge pins, service bars, rings, even lapel flowers, all have their personality and will help add to yours. Sometimes, too, they serve to attract the eye to the extent that you, personally, are not scrutinized. How many times have you read descriptions in the paper where a witness says, "Well, he had a red flower in his button hole, and I think a sort of grayish suit, but I'm not sure." The flower had caught the eye to the exclusion of all else. This same principle can apply just as well to spectacles, a tie, a mustache or the way you wear your hat.

Prepared Quick Changes

Being familiar with both "quick changes" and "*prepared* quick changes" has definite advantages. You have a reserve of ideas that may be very useful. Furthermore, many elements of chance are eliminated, while speed and superior results are made possible.

If at all possible work with another student. Report to him in exactly the clothes you expect to wear in the field. Ask him to study you as a whole first, then go to details.

Just what particular points about your appearance struck him first? Make notes as you go, so that you do not become accustomed to those points and disregard them later. They are most likely the ones that the wrong person will notice also.

What did you do before the war? This might be a good lead as to what your change should be, as it will be easier for you to assume that character, physically and mentally, than any other. But be sure that it still makes you one of the crowd and fits the district you will be in.

If it is decided that you should change your complexion, get some skin color and see what can be done with it, following the instructions given in Chapter II [not included here].

If you decide you need a mustache, try on various samples of hairlace mustaches until you select the best one for size, shape and color to fit the character you are to become. (A hairlace is a net to which individual hairs are knotted.) The purpose of the mustache is not to make you look more handsome, but to hide or detract from some feature or to add authenticity, and it should be selected with that in mind. Properly put on, a hairlace becomes practically transparent and, except to close scrutiny, is unnoticeable even in broad daylight. Under normal conditions it will remain firmly stuck, if applied correctly, for at least two or three hours. Detailed instructions are given in Chapter II [not included].

A good precaution is to practice putting on the mustache *by feel*, without the aid of a mirror, until you can get it on straight and quickly every time. Establishing three points on the upper lip in relation to the particular mustache will make this possible: (1) the part must be equally centered on the lip, and (2) the right distance below the center of the nose; and (3) the two ends must be equally distant above the corners of the mouth. Keep trying this until you can do it almost automatically. Nothing will catch the eye quicker than a lopsided mustache.

Spectacles should definitely be considered as a possible aid in your disguise. This subject also is discussed in Chapter II [not included here].

If it is decided that you need a second identification card or papers, make yourself up as you expect to look and have the necessary photograph taken. Several questions, however, should first be answered. Should the photograph look like one made when you were younger? Should it be taken in a different suit? Should a slightly different style of haircut or mustache (if one is to be worn) be used?

Learn how to hide your necessary disguise materials, bearing in mind that you must have them on your person. (Articles are hidden mainly to keep them from prying landlords and curious small-town officials.) Spirit gum and skin color can easily be concealed, for example, in small glass vials inside cigarettes.

Your second identification card and your hairlace mustache can be kept in your cigarette or spectacle case. Care must be exercised, however, not to flatten the hairlace, since it is the "dressing" or shape that makes it look real.

When you practice assuming your complete disguise, you should work in a prearranged sequence, doing the most important things first, in case you do not have time to finish the job.

Women Students

While many of the suggestions outlined in this volume are applicable to both men and women students, the following section is written solely for the women.

A change of hair style is one of the most simple and effective aids in changing a woman's appearance. If the usual style, for instance, is a "long bob", the hair should be done up, or slicked straight back into either a knot or a roll. The position of the part should be altered or eliminated altogether. If the hair is usually worn closely set, brushing it out frizzy and adding a ribbon bow will create a different effect immediately. The advisability of taking along a switch, either to add more hair or to use as a braid, should be considered. The style chosen should be one that a woman can arrange herself, naturally, without recourse to a beauty parlor. An important point to remember is that the most unbecoming hair style will probably change the wearer's appearance more than any other.

It should be borne in mind that in many parts of the world women do not get or use much make-up. If lipstick is used, however, making a different lip line will alter the appearance greatly, as will changing the shape of the eyebrows.

If a woman does not want to be noticed, she should strive to look mousy or old or dumpy. If the work calls for glamour, an expert on make-up should be consulted.

A woman who normally chooses bright and colorful clothes should change to something darker, say a grey dress or suit. The point is to achieve a complete contrast from the clothes usually worn.

A woman of between thirty and forty years of age can easily add ten to fifteen years to her apparent age after a little instruction. She should clean off all make-up, wrinkle up her face, and with a very sharp Factor's brown eyebrow pencil lightly line all of the creases. Rub these down to the point where they are only soft shadows. A very thin application of the brown pencil mixed with Factor's No. 6 blue-grey liner, close to the bridge of the nose and accentuating the circles under the eyes, will add to the effect. Next, a light-colored make-up should be used on all the high spots – the cheek bones, nose, chin and the tops of all wrinkles, care being taken to blend all edges out to nothing. Patting the face lightly all over will help do this. Remember, it is shadows and highlights which are being added, and they must be soft so as to look completely natural. A fairly light powder should be applied, patted well in first, then brushed off as much as possible. Next a damp cloth should be used to remove all the excess powder. If any lipstick is used at all, it should be thin and light-colored and blotted off. Next, the lips should be puckered and powder added on top of the lipstick.

If the student wears dental plates or removable bridges, she should take them out. The neck and hands must not be overlooked; all must tie in together. A little hair white should be combed in at the temples or streaked through the whole head and the hair done up in an older style. When the make-up is all finished, the details should be checked. If she looks made-up at all, the job has been overdone. The materials were probably used too thick or not blended enough. Students will find that a little practice before a mirror will produce excellent results.

A change of dress into something somber and without shoulder padding comes next. Clothes cut to the lines of the figure should be avoided. By not wearing a girdle a youthful-appearing figure can often be changed. A larger brassiere and padding the bust, or even a padded girdle, should be considered. A pair of low-heeled shoes will alter the student's walk. For other suggestions on posture and gait, consult the section on this subject above.

STEN GUN MANUAL, 1944

SMALL ARMS TRAINING, VOLUME 1, PAMPHLET NO. 21

The War Office

The Sten gun was the quintessential weapon of the Allied resistance fighter. It was very simple; very cheap; used a common type of 9mm pistol ammunition that could be supplied from the UK or captured from the enemy; was powerful at close range, and was manufactured in huge numbers. As a weapon of SOE it had the particular virtue of compactness for air drops and concealment, though on the downside its magazine feed could be damaged by poor handling. About a million Sten guns were distributed by SOE. Eventually it would see service in partisan and clandestine actions as diverse as the Warsaw Rising of 1944, and Maquis fights in Brittany. Its basic characteristics made it ideal for urban actions, and in the Warsaw Rising members of the Polish 'Home Army' are recorded as having advanced to their start points carrying their Stens under their jackets before opening the battle. At the same time the Sten equipped the British regular army in every theatre of war.

The name 'Sten' was derived from the initials of the designers Major R. V. Shepherd and H. J. Turpin, and the first two letters of 'Enfield'. The gun had a 32-round detachable box magazine, and worked on a 'blow back' system. There were six slightly different basic models, including one with a silencer.

As supplied by SOE it usually came broken down into three pieces, with three or four full magazines. Instructions were supplied in a variety of languages, but the Sten was so simple that these were scarcely necessary. Indeed, with even a modicum of practice, it is possible to assemble a Sten, quite literally, blindfolded. Remarkably the Germans even produced a copy of the Sten for use by their own irregular forces.

SECTION 2.–THE STEN MACHINE CARBINE
LESSON 1.– LOADING AND UNLOADING

Instructor's notes

Stores:– Sten machine carbine with sling fitted; magazines.

All parts will be named as dealt with (Plate 6).

Live ammunition may be used for teaching magazine filling ONLY.

Its use must be carefully supervised and in no circumstances will it be used for any other purpose.

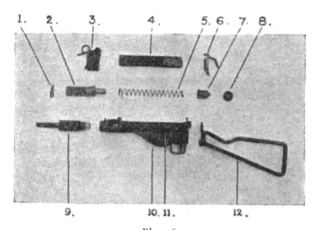

Plate 6

Key to Plate 6

1. Cocking handle.
2. Bolt.
3. Magazine filler Mark I.
4. Magazine.
5. Recoil spring.
6. Magazine filler Mark IV.
7. Recoil spring housing.
8. Recoil spring cap.
9. Barrel and barrel nut,
10. Body.
11. Stud.
12. Butt.

1. Explain general notes, para. 3.

2. Magazine filling.

(a) Explain and demonstrate:– The magazine spring is too

powerful to enable filling to be done quickly by hand; a filler is, therefore, provided. The most common is the Mark IV filler.

To fit the filler: Hold the magazine with the groove towards the body; keeping the nose of the filling lever clear, place the filler over the magazine so that the tongue on the filler fits into the rectangular recess in the magazine. Slide the filler upwards till it engages. If it does not engage easily, lift the filler spring.

To fill the magazine: With the left hand raise the lever to depress the magazine platform. Pick up a convenient number of rounds in the right hand and see that they are clean. Insert a round, base first, *under* the lips of the magazine (NEVER try to force a round downwards between the lips, or they may be damaged.) Lower the filling lever and push the round fully home. Repeat these actions, counting the rounds while filling. The magazine holds 32 rounds. To remove the filler, lift the spring, and slide the filler downwards and off.

Note.– The Sten will fire most makes of 9 mm. ammunition, including German and Italian,

(b) *To empty.*– Remove each round with the thumb and forefinger.

(c) Practise squad.

Note.– The Mark I filler, shaped like a box with a brass lever, may occasionally be met. In this case, fill the magazine as follows:–

Place the filler over the magazine so that the catch on the filler spring engages with the rectangular recess on the magazine. Hold the magazine with the groove pointing away from the body; place the fingers of the left hand on the filling lever with the forefinger through the loop. Press down the lever to depress the magazine platform. Insert a round base first, under the nose of the lever; raise the lever quickly up and down to guide the round into place. Repeat these actions till the magazine is full, making certain that each round is guided into place under the lips. (To remove the filler, raise the spring and lift off.)

3. Loading, "ready" position, and unloading.

(a) Explain and demonstrate with an empty magazine:–

To load.– Hold the Sten with the right hand on the butt grip, forefinger outside the trigger guard, butt under the arm, and barrel pointing to the front and downwards. Pull back the cocking handle and move it into the safety slot at the top of the carbine. Take the magazine in the left hand, with the groove to the rear, look to see that the top round is in the correct position (Plate 7 [not included here]), then insert the magazine into the housing on the left side of the carbine. *See that it is fully home.*

Carriage. – The Sten can be carried:–

    (i) Slung over the shoulder,

    (ii) At the trail, like the rifle,

    (iii) In front of the body with the sling round the neck.

When the enemy is likely to be met, the "ready" position can quickly be adopted from any of these positions as follows:–

Bring the weapon close in to the right side with the butt under the arm and the barrel pointing to the front. Release the cocking handle from the safety slot, grasp the barrel nut with the left hand well clear of the ejection opening and the wrist under the magazine, and put the right forefinger on the trigger.

To unload. – Return to the loading position. Depress the catch on the magazine housing with the thumb and remove the magazine. Holding the cocking handle with the left hand, press the trigger and ease the working parts forward under control. Cock and ease the working parts forward again.

Note.– If the working parts are forward with a full or partially full magazine in the housing, a round may be fired if the Sten is suddenly jerked or the cocking handle is released prematurely during cocking. The cocking handle, therefore, must *always* be in the safety slot before a magazine is put on the weapon.

(b) Practise squad. (Words of command: "Load" – "Slung position," etc. "Ready" – "Unload".)

4. The sights.

Explain :– The Sten is fitted with a fixed aperture backsight for ranges up to 100 yards. The rule for aiming is as for the L.M.G.

LESSON 2. – FIRING

Instructor's notes
Stores:– Sten machine carbine with sling fitted; magazines; three Fig. 2 [not included here] targets.
The breech should be padded with a wad of cotton waste or paper, to prevent damage to the bolt when the trigger is pressed.

1. Firing positions.

Explain:– There are three methods of firing the Sten, as follows:–

(a) From the shoulder, using the sights as taught. (Plate 8 [not included here]).

(b) From the shoulder, roughly aligning the barrel on the enemy, but without using the sights.

(c) From the waist, by sense of direction. (Plate 9 [not included here]).

The position used will depend on the circumstances. Always use the sights if time permits, and fire from the waist only when speed is of great importance. In an emergency fire can be applied from the waist on the move, but if it is possible to halt momentarily, greater accuracy will result.

2. Types of fire.

Explain:– The type of fire can be altered by moving the stud on the trigger mechanism casing. By pressing in the side marked "R" the Sten will fire single rounds; if the side marked "A ", it will fire bursts.

Normally the Sten will be fired in bursts, and in the field the stud should be set at "Automatic". Bursts should rarely be of more than 2 or 3 rounds. There will be occasions, however, when single rounds, fired from the shoulder, will be sufficient to deal with the enemy.

3. Firing.

Explain and demonstrate from the "ready" position:–

(a) *Firing from the shoulder, using the sights.*–The position and method of firing is the same as for the rifle, except that the enemy should be faced squarely. When the enemy has been dealt with, continue to advance at the "ready" position. If the enemy is not likely to appear again, put the cocking handle in the safety recess. In either case change the magazine if necessary.

Practise squad at the halt and on the move, emphasizing the need for speed in coming into action. (Words of command:– "Load" – "Ready" – "Fire," etc. – "Unload"). The Sten should be re-cocked each time after firing.

(b) *Firing from the shoulder, roughly aligning the barrel.* – When the enemy appears, swing the body from the waist, at the same time bringing the Sten into the shoulder and quickly pointing the muzzle at the enemy. The position of the feet is immaterial, provided that balance can be maintained. While firing, observe the strike of shots if possible, and correct the alignment of the barrel as necessary.

Practise squad as in *(a)*. (Words of command: "Load" – "Ready" "Target right", etc.– "Fire" – "Miss low," etc. – "Advance"). The instructor must check for direction.

(c) *Firing from the waist.* – Swing the body from the waist as before, and fire straight from the "ready" position. Since firing is entirely by sense of direction, every effort should be made to observe results. Practise squad as in *(b)*.

Note. – Whenever possible full use should be made of the spotlight projector *(see* Appendix B). This enables the instructor to check, and the firer to see his own mistakes.

4. Immediate action.

(a) Explain and demonstrate. – If the Sten fails to fire or stops firing, cock it and look quickly into the ejection opening. If the magazine is empty, change it and go on firing. If there are rounds in the magazine, push it fully home and go on firing.

Practise squad. (Words of command : "Sten fires all right" – "Sten stops" – "Magazine empty "or "Rounds in magazine" –"Sten fires all right").

(b) If, after cocking and looking in the ejection opening, there is an obstruction, turn the Sten to the right and shake vigorously; the round or empty case should fall out. If it does, and the chamber is clear, go on firing. If the obstruction is still there, or if there is a live round in the chamber, partially remove the magazine and clear the obstruction by shaking or the live round by firing. Cock if necessary, re-engage the magazine, and go on firing.

(c) A misplaced round in the magazine will be flicked out and any round half-fed in the chamber or in the body shaken out; and in neither case will the round be replaced in the magazine. These rounds will be regarded as damaged, whether any signs are visible or not, and as such will be rejected.

Note. – In darkness feel inside the ejection opening to make certain that the obstruction has been removed.

Practise squad, (Words of command : "Sten fires all right" – "Sten stops" – "Obstruction" – "Clear" – "Live round in chamber", etc. – "Sten fires all right").

5. Safety precautions when firing the Sten.

If the Sten cannot be cocked by hand, remove the magazine, loop a cord or pull-through round the cocking handle and give it a sharp jerk to release it. Carry out the normal immediate action, making certain for safety reasons that the barrel is pointing towards the target.

LESSON 3.–STRIPPING AND CLEANING

Instructor's notes
Stores :– Sten machine carbine; magazine; pull-through; flannelette and oil; gauze.
For names of parts, see Plate 6.

1. Stripping.

Explain and demonstrate:–

(a) Cock the Sten and ease the working parts forward. This must always be done before any part is stripped.

(b) *Butt.* – Press in the stud on the recoil spring housing and slide the butt downwards and off.

(c) *Bolt.* – Press the cap (or ring) round the stud inwards and turn it anti-clockwise; this will unlock it from its seating in the body. Remove the cap, spring housing, and spring. Draw the cocking handle to the rear, turn it halfway into the safety slot, and remove it. Slide the bolt out of the body.

(d) *Barrel (Marks II and V only).* – Pull out the plunger on the side of the magazine housing and turn the housing downwards. Unscrew the barrel and barrel nut (the front hand grip) together and remove.

The Sten will **not** be stripped further than this except to rectify damage.

2. Assembling.

Explain and demonstrate:–

(a) *Barrel.* – Push the barrel on to its seating and screw the barrel nut partially home, Make certain that the line or the three figures on the barrel are roughly in line with the foresight (inaccurate shooting will result if this is not done). Screw the barrel nut fully home and turn the magazine housing back to its normal position.

(b) *Bolt and spring.* – Hold the Sten horizontally and push the bolt into the body; then, keeping the trigger pressed, push it forward until the hole for the cocking handle is opposite the safety slot. With one end of the cocking handle as a guide, bring the hole into the correct position and insert the cocking handle. Keep the trigger pressed and slide the bolt forward. (Never *drop* the bolt into the body vertically; the ejector may be damaged.) Insert the spring and its housing, replace the cap, press it into its slots and turn it clockwise until it engages.

(c) *Butt.* – Press the stud on the recoil spring housing inwards with the top of the butt. Hook the butt catch into its slide, and push upwards till the butt is locked. Cock and test the action.

3. Practise squad.

4. Stripping the magazine
Explain and demonstrate:–

(a) *Stripping.*–Press in the stud on the bottom plate and slide it off, controlling the spring as it comes out. Lift out the spring and platform.

(b) *Assembling.*–Replace the platform and spring, and slide on the bottom plate until the stud engages in the hole in the plate. A tap with the hand will help it to engage.

5. Cleaning.

(a) Explain and demonstrate:– Strip the Sten completely. Clean the bore as taught for the rifle, using the pull-through and flannelette size 4 ins. by 3 ins. A gauze is provided but should be used only when absolutely necessary. When the bore is clean, oil it, using flannelette size 4 ins. by 2 ins. Clean and oil the chamber, using the pull-through weight or a piece of stick with flannelette placed on it. Thoroughly clean and oil the rest of the weapon, paying special attention to the following:–

The face of the bolt.

The inside of the body and the ejector.

Note. – Before firing the weapon should be completely dry if possible. Unlike the Thompson, the Sten will fire whether dry or oily, but in hot dry climates all oil must be removed before firing.

Clean the magazines with an oily rag. Make certain that the inside of each magazine is perfectly clean and contains no rough projections; also examine the lips to see that they are not damaged. If ammunition is available, make certain that the top round is at the correct angle (see Plate 7 [not included here]).

Finally test each magazine in the magazine housing to ensure that it will fit.

(b) Practise squad.

6. Decontamination.

(a) Explain that if the Sten becomes contaminated by gas it should be cleaned like the rifle (*see* Pamphlet No. 3, lesson 1 [not included here]).

(b) Question squad.

QUICK USE OF THE STEN GUN

This illustration shows the supporting hand gripped under the barrel, and the body leaning slightly forward. Best results were achieved from the shoulder in very short bursts.

PICTURE CREDITS

Front endpapers and first plate section taken from *Descriptive Catalogue of Special Devices and Supplies, 1944*. Back endpapers and second plate section taken from *Descriptive Catalogue of Special Devices and Supplies, 1945*. All reproduced by permission of The National Archives.

All other illustrations from the author's collection.

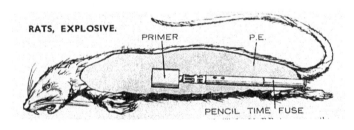

THE SOE EXPLODING RAT

This ingenious device consisted of a real animal skin stuffed with explosives. The ideas was that the carcass should be left near boilers – perhaps amongst fuel – in factories, power stations, or other enemy installations. As soon as it was shovelled into the flames it would detonate, spreading fire and wrecking machinery. Similar items available included explosive coal and logs.

PORTABLE GRAMOPHONES.

The A. Mk. II wireless set fits conveniently into a continental type gramophone. By removing the gramophone motor, substituting a dummy spindle to carry the turntable, and cutting away the sound horn inside the gramophone, enough room is provided to take the four packs of the A. Mk. II wireless set.

This concealment is only for carrying purposes and the wireless set must be taken out of the gramophone and assembled for working. Wherever possible the gramophone is made to play and appropriate records are supplied. Plates below show details.

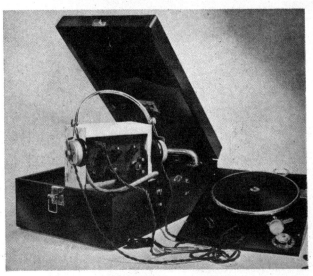